JEEP
WRANGLER JL & GLADIATOR JT
PERFORMANCE MODIFICATIONS

Don Alexander and Quinn Thomas

S·A DESIGN

CarTech®

CarTech®, Inc.
6118 Main Street
North Branch, MN 55056
Phone: 651-277-1200 or 800-551-4754
Fax: 651-277-1203
www.cartechbooks.com

Edit by Bob Wilson
Layout by Connie DeFlorin

ISBN 978-1-61325-595-7
Item No. SA503

Library of Congress Cataloging-in-Publication Data

Names: Alexander, Don, 1948- author. | Thomas, Quinn, 1971- author.
Title: Jeep Wranglerr JL and Gladiator JT : performance modifications / Don Alexander and Quinn Thomas.
Description: Forest Lake, MH : CarTech, Inc., [2021]
Identifiers: LCCN 2021026020 | ISBN 9781613255957 (paperback)
Subjects: LCSH: Wrangler sport utility vehicle. | Gladiator truck.
Classification: LCC TL215.W73 A5426 2021 | DDC 629.28/722--dc23
LC record available at https://lccn.loc.gov/2021026020

Written, edited, and designed in the U.S.A.
Printed in China
10 9 8 7 6 5 4 3 2 1

DISTRIBUTION BY:

Europe
PGUK
63 Hatton Garden
London EC1N 8LE, England
Phone: 020 7061 1980 • Fax: 020 7242 3725
www.pguk.co.uk

Australia
Renniks Publications Ltd.
3/37-39 Green Street
Banksmeadow, NSW 2109, Australia
Phone: 2 9695 7055 • Fax: 2 9695 7355
www.renniks.com

Canada
Login Canada
300 Saulteaux Crescent
Winnipeg, MB, R3J 3T2 Canada
Phone: 800 665 1148 • Fax: 800 665 0103
www.lb.ca

CONTENTS

ACKNOWLEDGMENTS

We first want to thank our wives, Christie Helm and Heather Thomas, for their support.

Thanks also to Bob Wilson, editor at CarTech; Corey and Casey, the All J Products crew; Bill Stephens for help with testing and installation; Wendy Stephens for testing and spotting help; Toby Jho for some great photos; Desi Hauer, Big Bear Jeep Experience; and Casey Sisson, JP Molnar for photo help.

And many thanks to our friends and associates in the awesome Jeep aftermarket: Ray Currie and Casey Currie, Currie Enterprises; John Currie, Brandon Currie, Brian Shepard, and Tiny Stark, RockJock 4x4; Paul Jho, Jay Lee, and John Hagen, Nexen Tires; Henk Van Dongen and Ryan Michael, Rugged Ridge; Tom Allen, PSC Motorsports; Neal Hollingsworth, Yukon Gear & Axle; Terry Jurgens, Ultra Vision Lighting; Greg Mulkey, Raceline Wheels; Steve Sasaki and Tyler Sasaki, Power Tank; Dave Luman, Kevin Smith, and Tom Trotter, Rock Slide Engineering; Jason Stanton, Tim Cowher, and Jon Mason, Novawinch; James Barth, Rock Hard 4x4; Justin Andrews, Factor 55; Shari McCullough Arfons, McCullough Public Relations and Tuffy Security; Jim Reel, JE Reel Drivelines; Steve von Seggern, Bilstein Shocks; Scott Brown, Fiat Chrysler Automobiles public relations; Henry Valesquez, BRP Wheels; Steve Dowden, Hi-Lift jacks; Don Sneddon and Willie Woo, Mickey Thompson Tires; Elizabeth Granada, Midland Radio Corp.; John and Cinde Angelastro, sPOD; Brittany and Kevin Williams, LiteBrite Nation; Jeff Greene, Rough Country; Gale Banks, Banks Power; Jason Buckles, Bolt Locks; Matson Breakey, MetalCloak; Dave Schlossberg, Synergy Manufacturing; Brad McCarthy, MaxTrax; Don McMillan, Daystar; and Max Gremillion, Pull Pal.

FOREWORD

By Paul Jho

Director of Motorsports and Events Nexen Tire America

I have always believed that passion is very important in life. It's different than just having a hobby. I also believe that having passion can resonate better with others. I am lucky to follow my passion in the automotive industry and do what I love. When you meet someone who has the same passion, that's when you know the friendship will be a great journey.

I wasn't familiar with the off-road industry until I went on a corporate ride and drive several years ago in Big Bear Lake, California. There, I met Don Alexander. We continued communicating afterward, and we later had the opportunity to work together when I moved to Nexen Tire America.

Don Alexander has racing experience from open-wheel Formula cars to driving at the Bonneville Salt Flats. He was hired to test our upcoming and first mud-terrain tire. Don is well connected in the off-road industry, and he introduced me to many great people in the industry, especially in the off-road segment. That was when I met Quinn Thomas and how he became part of our tire test program. Don and Quinn provided honest feedback and helped Nexen develop the new MT tire.

Don gave me a copy of the book that he wrote with Quinn about the Jeep JK, *Jeep Wrangler JK 2007–Present: Performance Upgrades* from CarTech, and I realized that all of the technical information in the book was actual data from the manufacturers—not just the opinion of Don or Quinn. Don's relationships with many of the company owners create a flow of accurate information. Both Don and Quinn have spent many hours installing various components and testing them on actual trails for this book.

Some people provide information based on sponsorships. In contrast, when Don and Quinn tell you what works and what doesn't based on testing and experience, you can make more informed decisions. They are clearly sharing great information with others.

I've learned so much from both Don and Quinn, ranging from the technical aspect of each component to driving on the trails. I've met their families, and their friendship has been meaningful to me. They brought new adventure into my life. Thanks to their Jeep JK book, I am currently the owner of a nice JKU that was built by Quinn and his staff. While observing the process of creating this book, I have been inspired to purchase a Jeep JT as my second rig.

Thank you to both Don Alexander and Quinn Thomas for opening up new adventures in my life and sharing so much with me. Also, thank you both for being so involved with Adopt-A-Trail and managing the program, which many don't realize is a critical part of maintaining and keeping our trails open.

Without passionate individuals such as Don and Quinn, we might not have all the great trails to create memories with close friends. Thank you again, and I hope the readers feel what I feel.

A NEW JEEP WRANGLER

The first Jeep Wrangler, the YJ, hit the market in 1987, 44 years after the first civilian Jeep, the CJ2, rolled off the assembly line. The last civilian Jeeps, the CJ7 and the CJ8 (Scrambler), looked similar to earlier versions of the CJ line.

Each model change saw some minor changes and upgrades. Jeep increased the size and offered more creature comforts. But every anticipated model change spurned rumors. How would the new model be different?

The changes always proved to be minor. The biggest visual alteration occurred when the first Wrangler hit the scene in 1987 with rectangular headlights. Every CJ model had round headlights that protruded slightly in the seven slots of the grille. When the Wrangler TJ appeared in 1996, the round headlights made a comeback. However, the headlights no longer protruded into the grille slots. In addition, the TJ featured coil springs and even more creature comforts.

In 2003, the first Jeep Wrangler Rubicon models appeared on the TJ. In 2004, Jeep gave the world a sneak peek into the future when the LJ Unlimited version of the TJ launched. While still a two-door model, the LJ Unlimited's longer wheelbase allowed improved comfort for rear seat passengers. It also altered the off-road dynamics of the platform.

Then, rumors began to fly. There was talk of a new Wrangler. How would it change from the TJ? Would it have independent suspension? What engine and transmission would be available? Would the seven-slot grille go away?

When the Jeep Wrangler JK debuted in 2007, it sort of looked like the TJ—sort of! It was much bigger,

The new Jeep Wrangler JL (right) and the Jeep Gladiator JT have far exceeded expectations and laid to rest many concerns that were raised by Jeep aficionados before the new models were released. The traditional Jeep look melds beautifully with modern technology. (Photo Courtesy FCA US LLC)

The Jeep heritage lives on with the Wrangler JL and Gladiator JT. Both vehicles feature several options for tops. All versions are easy to remove for that Jeep open-air experience. (Photo Courtesy FCA US LLC)

When a new Jeep Wrangler was announced in 2016, rumors were rampant. Would the new Wrangler JL have solid axles? Would it look like a Jeep Wrangler? Would it be as capable as the JK? It is even better than the JK. (Photo Courtesy FCA US LLC)

and a four-door version was offered: the JK Unlimited. Jeep purists believed that the size and changes would make the JK terrible off-road. However, it was the opposite. Sales skyrocketed and more aftermarket products became available for the JK than for any vehicle in history. An entire new market rushed to buy the new Wrangler and customize it.

By 2016, rumors surfaced about another new Wrangler. Once again, the rumor mill shifted into high gear (or maybe it was 4 low). Many Jeep aficionados believed that the new Wrangler would be graced with independent front suspension. Would the new model even look like a Wrangler? What engine would be used? In other words, how badly would Fiat

Another Jeep tradition lives on: both the Wrangler JL and Gladiator JT have removable doors. In addition, the windshields fold down. Jeep even includes a tool kit to easily facilitate door removal and windshield folding. (Photo Courtesy FCA US LLC)

The stock Wrangler JL Rubicon offers exceptional performance for the vast majority of off-road trails. The automotive aftermarket has jumped on board to create many products to enhance the appearance and off-road capabilities of the Wrangler JL and Gladiator JT. (Photo Courtesy FCA US LLC)

Chrysler Automobiles (FCA) screw up the Wrangler? FCA kept a very tight lid on the new model.

When the JK was in preproduction, aftermarket companies were able to purchase JKs to develop products. This was not the case when the new Wrangler JL went into production. Aftermarket companies waited like everyone else to acquire the new JL from Jeep dealers, with the exception of Mopar.

FCA wanted to gain an advantage on the aftermarket. Before the JL was launched, Mopar created a host of add-on JL parts to be sold through Jeep dealers, and the parts installed by the dealers were covered under FCA warranties.

When the Wrangler JL reached dealer showrooms, the multitude of questions were finally answered. The new JL looked very similar to the JK. The JL and JK were virtually identical in size. Suspension was the traditional (and preferred) solid axle, which helps make the Wrangler so capable off-road. The most noticeable visual alteration was the return

of headlights protruding into the seven-slot grille.

Massive mechanical changes elevated the JL to a true 21st-century SUV without losing any off-road capability. While the JK is comfortable, the JL takes luxury to new levels, at least for the Wrangler. While the venerable 3.6-liter V-6 is the base engine, a 4-cylinder, 2.0L turbo engine is a high-horsepower option. A 3.0L turbo diesel is now also available, and the new 8-speed automatic transmission is truly a game changer. Also, Jeep is finally offering a Hemi V-8.

Most of the rumors proved to be unfounded. Then came news of a long-anticipated Jeep pickup: the Gladiator JT. More rumors began to circulate. The Gladiator would be (choose one or more) too long, too heavy, have a poor breakover angle, have a terrible departure angle, be no good in the rocks, etc. Yes, the breakover and departure angles are less than ideal, but the Gladiator is surprisingly capable in the rocks and is a game changer for overlanding.

Major Differences: Wrangler JK versus Wrangler JL and Gladiator JT

The Jeep Wrangler JL maintains the traditional Jeep Wrangler look and persona. Except for some driveline carryover items, including the Pentastar V-6 engine and transfer cases, the JL is completely new. This is a look at the differences.

Exterior

At first glance, the JK and JL look very similar. The most obvious difference is the intrusion of the headlights into the grille. This feature reminds old-school Jeep owners of the CJ. A more tilted windshield improves aerodynamics but is visually subtle.

JL front and rear bumpers differ visually from the last JK model year.

The intrusion of the headlights into the seven-slot grille sets the Wrangler JL and Gladiator JT apart from the Wrangler JK. The CJ series also featured headlights that extended into the grille slots. The Rubicon model offers a metal front bumper as an option. The LED lights are also optional on all Wrangler and Gladiator models. (Photo Courtesy FCA US LLC)

The Sahara version of the Wrangler JL has chrome trim around the fog lights. Chrome grille inserts change the appearance of the JL. The Sahara is only available in the four-door Unlimited version in the Wrangler. (Photo Courtesy FCA US LLC)

The functional air vent at the rear of the front fenders is a unique feature on all of the Wranglers and Gladiators. The vent helps evacuate hot air from the engine bay. Flowing hot air away from the engine helps alleviate the cooling issues of the JK. (Photo Courtesy FCA US LLC)

The Wrangler JL features a longer wheelbase for both the two-door and Unlimited four-door versions when compared to the JK models. The front axle was moved forward to improve the approach angle and create more space in the interior. The Rubicon editions use hood-vent inserts to further improve cooling. (Photo Courtesy FCA US LLC)

New taillights enhance the look of the rear of the JL. The license plate was relocated from the body to the bumper. (Photo Courtesy FCA US LLC)

A steel bumper option is available on the Rubicon trim level. Hoods and body panels look different on the JL. Lighting upgrades improve nighttime operation. Optional light-emitting diode (LED) lighting is available on all trim levels.

The fender flares increase tire clearance on the Sport and Sahara trim levels. In addition, the Rubicon fenders increase tire clearance with raised mounts. Up to 35-inch tires will fit on the Rubicon with no modifications.

Interior

The Wrangler JK features a clean, comfortable, and functional interior. The JL interior takes a quantum leap in luxury and function. Even the base-model Sport offers more comfort and improved electronics.

The JL controls are arranged differently than the JK, and having more controls provides an enhanced driving experience both on- and off-road. Touch-screen electronics bring the Wrangler into the 21st century. Sound system options include an Alpine Premium Audio System and Sirius XM satellite radio.

If you were not aware that you were sliding behind the wheel of a Wrangler, you would think you entered a high-end luxury SUV. Comfortable seats (with leather as an option on the Rubicon) provide an enhanced driving experience both on- and off-road.

Mechanical

Jeep engineers made extensive efforts to improve fuel economy without sacrificing performance and safety. The JL Unlimited frame is about 100 pounds lighter than the JK. Five crossmembers are used to improve chassis rigidity. The wheel-base has been increased on both the two- and four-door versions by moving the front axle forward. This modification improved the approach angle.

Steep descents present a driving challenge. Wranglers and Gladiators that are equipped with an automatic transmission feature hill assist. Hill assist uses the on-board computer and the antilock braking system to control the descent speed when in four-wheel-drive low range. The speed of the descent is determined by the transmission gear in manual-shift mode. The lower the gear, the slower the speed. (Photo Courtesy FCA US LLC)

Open-air adventures with the top and doors removed are a unique tradition of Jeep Wranglers. The Gladiator shares the long-held Jeep heritage. A doorless and topless truck will grab attention anywhere. (Photo Courtesy FCA US LLC)

The suspension geometry is similar to the JK, but spring rates and shock tuning are improved for better ride and road feel. The various trim levels have different spring and

Towing capacity for an off-road-capable vehicle tends to be minimal. The Gladiator breaks that mold with a minimum towing capacity of 4,000 pound regardless of equipment. The Rubicon model with the Max Tow package and the 8-speed automatic transmission can tow 7,650 pounds. (Photo Courtesy FCA US LLC)

The Wrangler Sport comes with minimal accessories and upgrades compared to the Sahara and Rubicon models of both the Wrangler and Gladiator. The Sport model uses crank-up windows, and the base two-door Sport does not have air-conditioning as standard equipment. However, the Sport S has power windows and standard air-conditioning. The Sport and the Sport S with the 2.72:1 transfer-case ratio in low range provide adequate gearing for tires up to 40-inch diameter with gear-ratio changes in the axles. The Sport and the Sport S make excellent platforms for major builds, where axles, housings, suspension, and other items will be replaced anyway. (Photo Courtesy FCA US LLC)

shock combinations with the resulting changes to ground clearance. The Rubicon features the most aggressive suspension with the highest ground clearance.

Dana front and rear axles are used on all trim levels. The Rubicon axles are the new Dana 44 Advantek models that use thicker axle tubes for more rigidity; a smaller, stronger ring-and-pinion gearset for more ground clearance; and a wider track width of 62.9 inches front and rear.

The front axles on all trim levels feature a front-axle disconnect (FAD) that Wranglers have not had since the YJ. The YJ used a vacuum-operated system, whereas the JL uses a more robust and reliable electric disconnect. The FAD reduces wear on the front axle rotating components and improves fuel economy.

The Wrangler JL features aluminum steering knuckles powered by an electrohydraulic power-steering system. The JL uses an electric power-steering pump that provides a variable force to assist steering inputs in various conditions.

While the JL wheel lug pattern is still 5 on 5, the wheel lugs on the JL are 14 mm, which is slightly larger than on the JK. In addition, the JL uses hub-centric wheels as opposed to the lug-centric wheels on the JK. The JK uses different wheel specifications than the JK.

Brakes on the JL increased in size when compared to the JK. This offers improved braking performance, which is good news when upgrading to taller tires. The front brakes use 12.9 x 1.1-inch vented rotor with twin-piston floating calipers. The rear brakes use 13.4 x 0.55-inch solid rotors with single-piston floating calipers. An antilock braking system is used on all four wheels.

Drivetrain

Transfer cases on the JL are similar to the JK. The Sahara and the Sport editions use the MP3022 Selec-Trac transfer case with a 2.72:1 low-range ratio, whereas the Rubicon uses the NV241OR Rock-Trac transfer case with the 4.0:1 low-range ratio.

The biggest change on the JL is in the transmission lineup.

The game-changing automatic 8-speed transmission is standard on the 2.0L I-4 engine and 3.0L turbo diesel, and it is optional with the 3.6L

Vehicle	Transmission	Type	1st Gear	2nd Gear	3rd Gear	4th Gear	5th Gear	6th Gear	7th Gear	8th Gear	Reverse
JT	850RE TorqueFlite	automatic (8-speed with overdrive)	4.71	3.13	2.10	1.67	1.28	1.00	0.84	0.67	3.53
JT	D478	manual (6-speed with overdrive)	5.13	2.63	1.53	1.00	0.81	0.72	—	—	4.49
JK	NSG 370	manual (6-speed)	4.46	2.61	1.72	1.25	1.00	0.84	—	—	4.06
JK	42RLE	automatic (4-speed with overdrive, 2012–2018)	3.59	2.19	1.41	1.00	0.83	—	—	—	3.16

The JK transmissions are listed for comparison.

V-6. The 8-speed automatic transmission features adaptive electronic control or electronic range select (ERS), driver-interactive manual control and an electronically modulated torque-converter clutch.

The 6-speed manual transmission comes standard with the 3.6L V-6 Pentastar engine. The manual transmission comes synchronized in all forward gears and reverse, uses a multi-rail shift system with a top-mounted shift lever, and features a 50-percent shorter throw on the shifter.

The 8-speed automatic transmission in the JL is a game changer. With the super-low first gear, changing axle ratios becomes less critical when running tires up to 37 inches tall. First gear in the manual transmission for the JL is even lower. These low first-gear ratios offer high crawl ratios.

With the Rubicon trim level using the 4.0:1–ratio transfer in low range and first gear, the 8-speed automatic crawl ratio is 77.2:1, while the manual transmission ratio in the Rubicon is a huge 84.2:1. This compares to a 58.9:1 ratio in the JK with the automatic transmission and 73.1:1 with the manual transmission.

Wrangler JL crawl ratios with the MP3022 Selec-Trac transfer case with a 2.72:1 low-range ratio in low-range first gear are 53.5 with the automatic

transmission and 57.3 with the manual transmission.

Engine Options

Only the 3.8L V-6 was available for the Wrangler JK from 2007–2011. From 2012 forward, only the Pentastar 3.6L V-6 was available in the Wrangler. With five engine options for the Wrangler JL, the buyer has better, more interesting choices. Currently, the Gladiator JT offers the 3.6L Pentastar engine and a high-torque diesel.

The 3.6L Pentastar is still available in two versions: both a standard Pentastar and the eTorque system, which is a mild hybrid arrangement. The eTorque system comes as standard equipment on the 2.0L direct-injected, turbocharged inline-4 with 270 hp and 295 ft-lbs of torque.

The biggest news for the JL and JT is the 3.0L V-6 EcoDiesel, which became available in early 2020 on the JL and features 260 hp and 442 ft-lbs of torque. It also carries

a hefty price tag. The fuel economy numbers may make up for the cost. Even with a large amount of torque, the mileage improvement is impressive: 22 mpg city and 29 mpg highway. Mileage for the Pentastar V-6 is 17 city and 25 highway.

Trim Levels

If you are reading this book, chances are good that you know how capable the stock Wrangler and Gladiator models are, especially off-road.

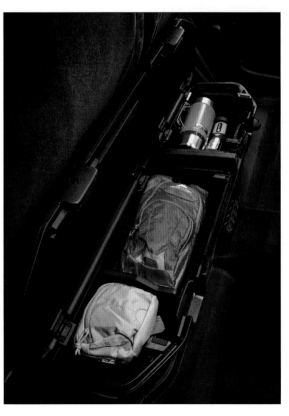

Gladiator JT owners have additional security even when the top and doors are removed with this locking compartment under the rear seat. (Photo Courtesy FCA US LLC)

The controls and electronics on both the Wrangler JL and Gladiator JT do not appear like equipment found on a rugged off-road vehicle. This Rubicon is equipped with the 8.4-inch touch-screen electronics, which includes an array of screens that offer a wide range of information and control. Climate controls and accessory switches are easy to reach and provide intuitive operation. A 12-volt outlet, window controls, and a media center with USB ports are below the climate controls and switches. The axle locker controls, sway-bar disconnect control, the off-road+ switch that activates the off-road touch screen, and four auxiliary switches round out the console. (Photo Courtesy FCA US LLC)

The performance differences between the models offer distinct options for the buyer, especially when off-road performance matters to the consumer. The important thing to determine is your goals for off-roading.

If off-road capability is of little or no importance, then budget and comfort will dictate the trim level and options. If off-road performance is important, especially if you plan to modify your Wrangler or Gladiator, then selecting the best trim level option is the key factor in the decision-making process. The Wrangler JL comes in three basic versions with several variations that change often. The Gladiator JT offers five models that also have variations.

Sport and Sport S Wrangler and Gladiator

The base model for both the Wrangler and Gladiator is the Sport. It has fewer options available. Off-road capability, while still better than most four-wheel-drive SUVs and trucks, leaves a lot to be desired compared to the Rubicon. Its creature comforts are minimal. For example, the Sport model uses manual window cranks. The two-door version has no air-conditioning as standard equipment. The Sport uses all-season tires on steel wheels and a

The Gladiator's rear seat folds into several configurations for a variety of storage options. (Photo Courtesy FCA US LLC)

standard suspension system that limits off-road performance.

The Sport S offers a few more amenities, including power windows. Alloy 17-inch wheels are standard. Air-conditioning is standard on both two- and four-door versions. Automatic headlights are also standard.

Wrangler Sahara Only

The Wrangler Sahara provides an improved interior and offers upgrades on the exterior when compared to the Sport and Sport S. The Sahara comes with 18-inch alloy wheels and all-season tires. The suspension upgrades provide more ground clearance. Many of the differences are cosmetic.

Overland and Mojave Gladiator Only

Both of these Gladiator versions are similar to the Wrangler Sahara with improved interior and exterior features. The Overland, as the name implies, is great for overlanding-style camping and exploration. The Mojave also features a suspension system designed for higher speeds on desert dirt roads, somewhat like the Ford Raptor.

Rubicon

The completely stock Wrangler Rubicon surpasses any other vehicle for off-road capability. The Gladiator outshines any other 4x4 truck for off-roading. Several features found only on the Rubicon models make a huge difference.
- Front and rear axle lockers
- Front sway-bar disconnect
- The NV241OR Rock-Trac transfer case with 4.0:1 low-range ratio
- 33-inch all-terrain or mud-terrain tires
- Dana 44 front and rear axles with 4.10:1 gear ratios

The Jeep 3.0L EcoDiesel engine is available in the Wrangler JL and the Gladiator JT. Power output is 260 hp and 442 ft-lbs of torque. Mileage is an impressive 22 mpg city and 29 mpg highway. (Photo Courtesy FCA US LLC)

- Higher fender profiles that accommodate larger tires

Experienced drivers can navigate trails, such as the famed Rubicon in Central California, with the stock Wrangler Rubicon. Damage is very possible, and the underside skidplates and stock rocker slides will get a workout, but traversing the Rubicon in a Rubicon is possible. In addition,

Jeep would be hard pressed to call a version of the Gladiator a Rubicon if it was unable to negotiate the Rubicon Trail. These Gladiator Rubicons are on the Rubicon. (Photo Courtesy FCA US LLC)

The Gladiator JT Overland Edition offers the perfect platform for overlanding adventures. A moderate lift and larger off-road tires can turn the Overland edition into an overland rig that is capable of tackling more than 90 percent of dirt roads and trails in the United States. (Photo Courtesy FCA US LLC)

the Rubicon has more bells and whistles than the other models.

Off-Road Use

How will you use your Wrangler or Gladiator off-road? Some options include casual, easy trails and dirt roads; overlanding on moderate terrain; difficult trails; extreme rock crawling; and desert exploration and camping.

Most first-time students at the Jeep 4x4 School want to learn how to use their new Jeep. Some feel that easy trails will be all they prefer to tackle. Others plan to make modifications for the more difficult trails. Still others plan to overland.

In nearly every instance, after being exposed to the capability of a stock Jeep, they plan to kick up the modifications a notch. More modifications are likely to be desired for your Jeep than were originally planned. If you are planning to buy a Wrangler, consider renting or test-driving a Wrangler before you buy.

Rocky trails are a breeze for the Gladiator JT Rubicon. The Sunrider Soft Top option on the lead Gladiator is optional on both the Gladiator JT and Wrangler JL. Access to open air is easy and quick. (Photo Courtesy FCA US LLC)

The Gladiator and Wrangler use a multifunction screen in the instrument cluster. This screen features pitch and roll angles. Knowing these angles can be both informative and scary! (Photo Courtesy FCA US LLC)

Hill climbs are fun challenges when off-roading. The Wrangler JL Rubicon tackles this 25-degree rutted slope with ease. (Photo Courtesy FCA US LLC)

The Gladiator is right at home in the Big Bear snow. Coauthor Quinn Thomas tackled snowy trails the first time his new Gladiator was off-road.

The Falken WildPeak A/T is one of our favorite all-terrain tires. This tire comes stock on the Gladiator Rubicon. (Photo Courtesy FCA US LLC)

Casual, Easy Trails and Dirt Roads

Any Wrangler or Gladiator will work well in these conditions. Adding off-road tires will make the lower-level models more capable. You can easily run 32-inch tires on the Sport models and 33-inch tires on the Wrangler Sahara and Gladiator Overland and Mojave editions with no modifications.

Overlanding on Moderate Terrain

The Wrangler Sahara with off-road tires, the Gladiator Overland or Mojave with larger off-road tires, and the Rubicon are great overlanding rigs on all but the most difficult trails.

Difficult Trails

The Rubicon models with minor modifications for both the Gladiator and Wrangler make tackling difficult trails a breeze. The Rubicon can run up to 35-inch mud-terrain or all-terrain tires without a lift. Running 37-inch tires will require at least a 2.5- to 3-inch lift.

Sand can be challenging, but the Gladiator looks at home here. (Photo Courtesy FCA US LLC)

Speculation that the Gladiator would not handle off-road has been proven unfounded. The Rubicon is on its home turf here. (Photo Courtesy FCA US LLC)

The Mojave edition of the Gladiator was designed for the higher speed and rough terrain of desert four-wheeling. The suspension is tuned for ruts, bumps, and whoops and high speeds across deserts. It can be compared to the Ford Raptor.

Wouldn't a Hellcat engine swap be a fun idea? (Photo Courtesy FCA US LLC)

The jury is still out concerning the durability of the stock Dana 44 axles in the Rubicon. Adding trusses and C-gussets to the axle housing will increase durability and longevity. Regearing is not necessary. Beefier skidplates are a good idea. Adding transmission and engine skids is a high priority.

Extreme Rock Crawling

Regardless of the model, considerable modifications are needed for extreme rock crawling. Building the JK for rock crawling pretty much required buying a Rubicon, mostly for the transfer case 4.0:1 low-range ratio. The option was to use an aftermarket transfer case, such as the Atlas. The JL offers more options.

With the extremely low first-gear ratios in the new 8-speed automatic transmission and the new 6-speed manual, it is no longer necessary to only consider a Rubicon. Even with the MP3022 Selec-Trac transfer case with a 2.72:1 low-range ratio, the crawl ratio is adequate for more extensive modifications, including axle gear ratio changes. A good portion of this book is devoted to these modifications.

If the plan is to run 40-inch tires (or larger), upgrade the following to ensure performance, reliability, and durability for extreme rock crawling:
- 4-inch-plus lift (preferably a long-arm design) with longer travel and more robust shock absorbers
- Stronger axle housing, axles, and gears (such as the Dana 60, Currie 60 Extreme, or Dynatrac 60)
- Complete underside skidplates
- Upgraded power steering with a hydraulic ram assist (PSC, Howe)
- Stronger tie-rod and drag link (RockJock Currectlync)

- Aftermarket fenders for additional tire clearance
- Aftermarket driveshafts (JE Reel, Tom Woods)
- Beadlock wheels (preferably)

If you plan to change all of these items, the Rubicon is no longer a necessity. The Sport (or Sport S for more comfort features) and the Sahara (Wrangler only) are great choices, and the cost is several thousand dollars less for the vehicle. It is possible to sell the take-off parts from a Rubicon to recoup some of the cost. But the hassle and risk makes it a tough choice.

Desert Exploration and Camping

Hands down, the Gladiator Mojave offers the best performance for the desert. The Mojave was designed for higher speeds and the ruts, bumps, and whoops that are found on desert dirt roads and trails. While any Wrangler or Gladiator can handle the terrain, the Gladiator Mojave will handle it better and easier.

Any Wrangler or Gladiator is a good choice if the Jeep will be used to explore, and any trim level can be easily modified for any off-road adventure desired. Planning ahead can save considerable time and money!

While most at home on sandy desert roads, the Gladiator Mojave can also handle rocks with ease. This is good because plenty of rocky sections litter desert trails. (Photo Courtesy FCA US LLC)

The Jeep Wrangler JL Rubicon lends itself to simple modifications for enhanced off-road capability. A 2.5-inch suspension lift is just right to run 37-inch tires without clearance issues.

MODIFICATIONS

The purchase of a new Jeep Wrangler or Gladiator is a big investment. Actually, investment may not be the most accurate word; expenditure is more realistic. However, the cost of a new Jeep is just the tip of the iceberg. After the purchase, modifications to a Wrangler or Gladiator are common for the vast majority of owners. If you have been down this road before, you know what you're up against. If you are a first timer building a Jeep, strap in tight! You are in for a ride rougher than the Rubicon Trail.

The large wad of cash that was spent to purchase a new Jeep can easily double by the time it has become a hard-core rock crawler. And that's if you have a plan and stick to it. Planning a Jeep build can seem like navigating a minefield for a newcomer. Overspending due to build mistakes is common. We speak from experience.

The task list for first-time Wrangler and Gladiator owners has an overwhelming number of choices. The first decision depends on how the Jeep will be used: easy trails, desert roads, mountain fire roads, moderate rock crawling, overlanding, extreme rock crawling, and/or mall crawling. Then, the owner must decide which modifications are needed to accomplish the desired goal.

Deciding which brands to use is daunting in and of itself. If you have traveled down this trail before, you likely have answers to all of the questions. However, if you're new to this, considerations prior to starting the build are invaluable.

The very first issue revolves around the off-road capabilities of the Wrangler and Gladiator. Many first-time owners attend the Jeep 4x4 School. Most of those owners have never driven off-road. The newcomer class begins with a half-hour drive on dirt roads to our training area. Most first timers are ecstatic about the new experience. While the students use four-wheel drive, it really is not necessary. Most students previously had no idea that such off-road opportunities even existed.

At the training site, the first obstacle is a 25-degree rutted climb that is followed by an equally steep

The Jeep Wrangler JL and Gladiator JT are great platforms for modification. This Gladiator JT began life as a Rubicon with significant modifications. This Wrangler JL began as a Sport S with many modifications. Selecting the best platform for your project requires research and some big decisions.

Even a stock Wrangler Sport S provides surprising performance off-road. Some minor modifications make a big difference in capability and reliability.

Newcomers quickly learn the capabilities of a Jeep Wrangler. This stock Sport S easily navigates a 25-degree hill at the Jeep 4x4 School in California.

The Wrangler and Gladiator lineups offer many trim and performance levels, and many dealers offer upgrades that can be included in the purchase and financed through the dealer. The Willys model JL offers some upgrades from the factory. The dealer added a small lift and upgraded wheels and tires. Many Jeep dealers make modifications and include them in the warranty.

rock-crawling climb. Any Wrangler or Gladiator can negotiate the course fairly easily, at least in dry conditions.

When we head for the first climb, the common reaction is, "We're going up *that*?"

Although attendees can see only treetops and sky on the ascent, their Jeeps easily make the climb with the guidance of a facilitator. If the student had any previous doubts about the purchase, those doubts vanish in a few feet of steep dirt incline, as the anxiety turns to elation. Facial stress morphs into large smiles. The sensation intoxicates the driver.

On the pre-class questionnaire, we ask students about their experience and how they plan to use their Jeep. Exploring, camping, and driving easy-to-moderate trails are common answers. We also ask how they plan to modify their Jeep. The installation of a suspension lift, bigger tires, lights, bumpers, fenders, and a winch are prevalent answers.

After 10 minutes of driving up and down steep hills, climbing over big ruts and bumps, and navigating minor rock obstacles, the original plan usually flies out the window. At the first break, questions flow. Minimal experience compressed into a few minutes alters the perspective of the newcomer. Almost without exception, the student looks at more extensive modifications.

While more modifications translate into more cost, the student will save money in the long run by completing a build only once. The individual who planned to tackle nothing more than moderate trails would now like to take on more difficult terrain. We haven't heard students say that they plan to make fewer modifications and upgrades. So, what modifications and gear are needed?

The Key to Pandora's Box

Buying a Gladiator or a Wrangler is the key to Pandora's box. That box is unlocked the second that a new Jeep owner hits the dirt. Inside the box are opportunities—ways you never imagined to spend money. After all, JEEP is an acronym for "Just Empty Every Pocket!" . . . and then some. Purchasing a $50,000 Jeep often means spending that same amount on modifications and upgrades, and it could mean spending even more if you really go for the ultimate overlander.

Most of this book is devoted to helping you make decisions about what modifications to make and which products are a good value. Regardless of the planned use of a Wrangler or a Gladiator, or which model is used, here are nine must-have items to carry for off-road adventures:

- First-aid kit
- Fire extinguisher
- Tow strap

Jeep Wrangler JL and Gladiator Build Goals

TECH TIP

- Improve off-road performance
- Minimize negative effects on highway performance and fuel economy
- Increase ground clearance without raising the center of gravity too much
- Personalize the appearance and function of the Jeep
- Provide adequate underside protection for key components
- Protect expensive body panels from damage as much as possible
- Improve system reliability to minimize the risks of trail breakdowns

A spacer lift and 35-inch-diameter tires allows the Gladiator Rubicon to negotiate black-diamond trails, including Gold Mountain, which is a Jeep Badge of Honor trail.

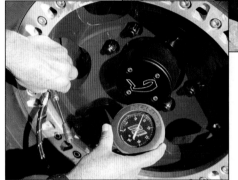

Tire pressures play a key role in off-road performance and comfort. Reducing tire pressure or "airing down" tires improves both traction and ride quality off-road. A tire deflator, such as the RockJock Deflator, provides an inexpensive way to lower tire pressure quickly.

- Shackles
- Communication device (ham radio, CB radio, cell phone, satellite radio, satellite tracker)
- Tire deflator for airing down
- Air compressor for airing up
- Front sway bar disconnect (not needed for Rubicon models)
- Upgraded off-road tires (mud-terrain or all-terrain not needed for Rubicon models)

The cost for the above modifications and upgrades is about $2,000.

For moderate trails, get all of the above plus:

- 35-inch-tall mud- or all-terrain tires

- Wider wheels
- 2–3-inch suspension lift (not needed on Rubicon models)
- Engine and transmission skidplate
- Rock sliders
- Bumpers
- Fenders
- Winch
- Regearing for non-Rubicon models
- Axle Lockers (rear minimum) for non-Rubicon models

The cost for the above modifications and upgrades is about $7,500 to $10,000 plus $2,000 for the first list.

For overlanding, get all of the first category plus:

- Food storage (protected)
- Water storage
- Cold storage (ice chest or refrigerator)
- Sleeping accommodations (sleeping bags)
- Shelter (stand-alone tent, rooftop tent, or trailer)

The cost for the above modifications and upgrades is about $700 to $10,000 plus $2,000 for the first list.

For more difficult rock crawling trails, such as the Rubicon, include everything from the first section and:

- 37-inch tires
- Wider wheels with less backspacing

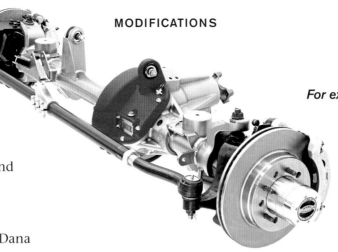

For extreme rock crawling, after-market axle assemblies, such as the Currie 60 Extreme front axle, improves performance and reliability.

- Full 4-inch lift kit with stronger control arms and joints and high-performance shock absorbers
- Stronger track bars, tie-rod, and drag link
- Hydraulic ram–assist steering damper
- Aftermarket axle assemblies (Dana 44–based at minimum) or stronger axle shafts and axle housing trusses and C-gussets
- Aftermarket driveshafts
- Rock sliders
- Bumpers
- Fenders
- Winch
- Regearing for non-Rubicon models
- Full underside skidplate system

The cost for the above modifications and upgrades is about $21,000 to $30,000 plus $2,000 for the first list.

For extreme rock crawling, such as the Hammers and Sand Hollow in Utah, include all from the first section and:

- 40-inch tires
- Beadlock wheels with less backspacing
- Full 4-inch lift kit with stronger control arms and joints and high-performance shock absorbers with remote reservoirs
- Stronger track bars, tie rod, and drag link
- Complete hydraulic steering system, including steering box, pump, ram assist, lines, and cooler
- Aftermarket axle assemblies (Dana 60–based at minimum) with big brakes and axle lockers
- Aftermarket driveshafts
- Rock sliders
- Bumpers
- Fenders
- Winch

Axle articulation is extremely important off-road. Even with a minimal build, installing a front sway-bar quick disconnect allows full axle articulation. Even easy trails have large bumps and ruts, necessitating good axle flex.

- Heavy-duty battery
- Full underside skidplate system
- Additional lighting
- Bolt-in sport roll cage for added safety
- On-board compressor

The cost for the above modifications and upgrades is about $45,000 to $55,000 plus $2,000 for the first list.

A simple spacer lift on a Gladiator Rubicon allows the use of 37-inch-diameter tires. Holcomb Creek is a Jeep Badge of Honor trail in Big Bear Lake, California, that offers serious challenges for the moderate modifications on the Gladiator. (Photo Courtesy Toby Jho)

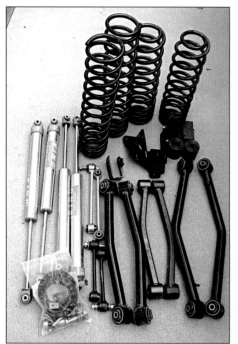

The Superlift 4-inch lift for the JL with premium King shocks provides great off-road performance for a reasonable cost. The kit includes lift springs, control arms, sway-bar links, brackets, and hardware.

Extreme rock crawling requires a strong suspension system. The Rockjock Sport Edition 4-inch JL suspension lift provides excellent durability combined with great off-road performance and flex.

Full flex over rough terrain requires good suspension and shock absorbers as well as tires at a lower pressure. The RockJock 4-inch lift with Bilstein bypass shocks works incredibly well on rough, rutted, and bumpy surfaces. The Nexen Roadian MTX tires run at 14 psi off-road for improved traction and a better ride.

Underside protection keeps important components from trail damage. The Artec aluminum skidplate system on a Gladiator provides superior protection when compared to the stock skidplates and adds very little weight.

Shock absorbers play a key role in off-road performance. Shocks also affect ride quality, which is an important characteristic of good shocks. The Bilstein B8 8100 bypass shock absorbers perform exceptionally well and offer a wide range of adjustment. While they are expensive, the performance and durability are worth the investment.

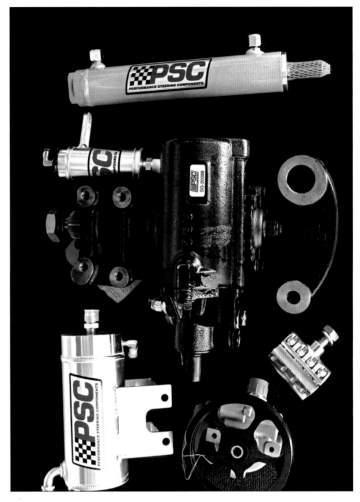

Aftermarket bumpers add protection and style to the Jeep Gladiator JT and Wrangler JL. Dozens of front bumpers, such as the Metalcloak frame-built bumper, allow for a custom look to any Wrangler or Gladiator.

The power-steering system on the Wrangler JL and Gladiator JT uses an aluminum steering box and an electric power-steering pump. The stock steering has proven to be problematic. PSC offers the Big Bore replacement steering system for the Wrangler JL and Gladiator JT. The PSC steering is stronger and makes steering a breeze in the most extreme conditions.

Rock sliders provide extra protection for the rocker panels in rocky terrain. Rock Slide Engineering makes a bulletproof slider with a built-in retractable step. Climbing in and out of a lifted Jeep can be a challenge. The Rock Slide Engineering Slider Steps make ingress and egress a breeze.

The Rugged Ridge HD rear bumper provides protection and convenience. The heavy-duty bumper is easy to install even in a driveway.

Items to Consider

If you are a complete newcomer to Jeeping, start with the first list. You need all of that gear anyway. Gaining some experience before leaping into a more expensive build will help you make a sound decision concerning the desired off-road use of your Jeep. You may be perfectly content with this level of off-road performance. Any appearance and convenience upgrades can be added at any time.

If you want to go overlanding, try it with some basics first. Nearly all of the gear needed to overland can be added at any time. Planning a build for moderate rock-crawling adventures creates more difficult decisions. Nearly everyone I know (including myself) who has built a Jeep for more moderate wheeling has decided to go extreme. While that is not the end of the world, it will add to the cost.

For example, upgrading to axle assemblies with Dana 44–based aftermarket units or adding trusses, stronger axle shafts, and gussets, is a considerable investment in upgrades. This setup will not live long in the extreme environment of hard-core rock crawling.

The upgrade to Dana 60 (or stronger) aftermarket axles is expensive. While some money can be recouped by selling the old axles, you will lose some of the investment. If the goal is to tackle moderate rock crawling, consider going all in with the extreme setup if you can afford the initial outlay. You will save money in the long run.

As we progress through the chapters, we delve into the specifications that are required to create a Jeep Wrangler JL or a Gladiator JT that will suit your needs. In addition to the key elements of a build that are outlined here, we will also cover less-essential upgrades that will enhance off-road adventures and personalize your Jeep.

Back in the days of the CJ and even the early Wrangler YJ, not many upgrades were available. Many parts were custom made. Today, the opposite is true. Jeep enthusiasts have an abundance of choices. More parts are available for Jeeps than any other brand in the history of the aftermarket. We'll show many ways to enhance a project Jeep while helping keep some money in your pockets.

Aftermarket fenders alter the look of a Wrangler or Gladiator. The Rugged Ridge Steel Tube Fenders increase tire clearance and are much stronger than the stock fenders.

SUSPENSION

Selecting a suspension lift kit can be daunting, especially for a newcomer. A variety of lift heights, suspension designs, and other factors make selecting a suspension lift challenging.

Suspension lift heights must be coordinated with tire diameter. Tire rub will occur, especially in extreme articulation situations, when there is too little lift for a given tire size. If the lift is taller than necessary, the elevated center of gravity can make a Jeep less stable on the highway and more prone to rollovers on the trails. Ideally, a suspension lift should be only as tall as needed to fit the desired tire diameter.

The combination of larger tires and taller suspension increases ground clearance, which allows easier passage over rough terrain. Keep in mind that a suspension lift raises the frame and body, but the axle housings are still the low point of the vehicle. Only taller tires will increase clearance under the axle housings.

Suspension lifts allow the fitment of taller tires. The increased clearance comes from taller springs. It may sound simple enough, but it's not so. Just making taller springs would be easy, but springs must be designed for height, suspension travel, and spring rate. Finding the optimum balance of spring rate, spring height, a level

Suspension systems play a key role in the performance of the Jeep Wrangler JL and Gladiator JT. Compromises are needed to create a package that has a good highway ride and handling along with exceptional off-road performance. This requires good engineering and practical experience. Not all suspension packages are created equally. (Photo Courtesy Toby Jho)

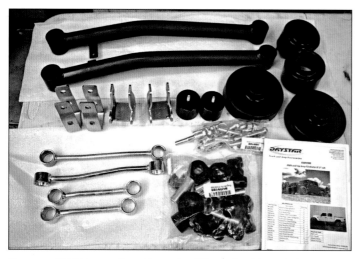

Spacer lift kits work well on the Wrangler JL and Gladiator JT to gain additional ground clearance without spending a fortune. They cost less than $400. The Daystar 2-inch spacer lift for the Gladiator includes polyurethane spacers, front lower control arms, sway-bar end links, extended bump stops, and front shock extensions. The Daystar spacer lift allows for the fitment of 37-inch tires on non-Rubicon models.

An aggressive lift kit with shock absorbers enhances ground clearance and allows for the use of 37-inch tires on non-Rubicon models while retaining the stock fenders. The Superlift 4-inch lift includes location-specific dual-rate coil springs, king shocks, compression-stop spacers (bump stops), extended sway-bar links, lower link arms, the track-bar bracket, hardware, and King 2.0 monotube gas shocks. Other shock options are available, including Superlift's Shadow Shocks or Fox 2.0 monotube shocks. The kit is also available with shock absorber extensions for use with the stock shocks.

The stock Wrangler JL and Gladiator JT models vary in ground clearance. The Rubicon models have more clearance than the Sport S version here. The Rubicon can run taller tires without a lift, but the other versions need a lift to fit tires that are 35 inches in diameter and above. The larger tires allow greater ground clearance.

The Gladiator Rubicon features Falken Wildpeak 33-inch tires from the factory. The Rubicon has good ground clearance, and the high-line fenders allow for the fitment of larger tires without a lift.

stance, and clearance requires good engineering and some trial-and-error testing.

Many suspension packages for the Wrangler JL and Gladiator JT use spring rates that are close to the factory stock rates to maintain a quality ride on the highway. Ride quality deteriorates when the springs are too stiff, and the vehicle wallows over rough surfaces if the springs are too soft.

Off-road, the chassis can bottom out if springs are too soft, and the rig will skate across rough surfaces if the springs are too stiff. Keep in mind that the most important job of the springs is to keep the tires planted on the road surface. Sway bars and shock absorbers are factors that are covered later in this chapter in greater detail.

The Wrangler JK needed a suspension lift to use tires larger than 33 inches in diameter. The JK had only one engine choice, and the suspension design was relatively simple. The Wrangler JL and Gladiator JT offer many more options for engines and running gear. Different models use various spring rates, and within a given model (Sport, Sahara, Rubicon), different engine options require different spring rates and shock valving.

To further complicate the design and manufacturing process for the Jeep aftermarket, the left and right front springs use different lengths and spring rates. In addition, the Rubicon models feature a raised fender line, which allows for the fitment of 35-inch-diameter tires with the stock suspension. A simple spacer lift on the Rubicon makes running 37-inch-diameter tires possible. The Sport and Sahara models require a lift kit and/or aftermarket fenders to fit tires larger than 33 inches in diameter.

Ground Clearance, Angles, and Center of Gravity

Lift kits increase the ground clearance under the body and the frame. They also allow the use of taller tires, which increases clearance under the lowest point of the axle housings.

Three angles crucial to off-road performance are also improved.

While the Jeep Wrangler JL has better angles than any other stock vehicle, increasing the angles improves off-road capability. Both a suspension lift and taller tires will improve these angles.

Jeep Wrangler JL Stock Angles				
Angle Type	Two-door Sport	Four-door Sport	Two-door Rubicon	Four-door Rubicon
Approach angle	41.4 degrees	41.4 degrees	44.0 degrees	43.9 degrees
Breakover angle	25.0 degrees	20.3 degrees	27.8 degrees	22.6 degrees
Departure angle	35.9 degrees	36.1 degrees	37.0 degrees	37.0 degrees

Approach, breakover, and departure angles determine the ability of a vehicle to clear larger obstacles. Bigger angles mean more clearance. The Gladiator in stock form has relatively small angles. Larger tires facilitated by a suspension lift improve the angles.

The Wrangler JL has better approach, departure, and breakover angles than the Gladiator JT due mostly to the shorter wheelbase and smaller rear overhang. The Rubicon has taller springs, which improve the angles.

A suspension lift kit, in this case a 4-inch lift and 40-inch-diameter tires, improves the approach, breakover, and departure angles considerably.

When a Jeep is lifted, the center of gravity is elevated. A higher center of gravity increases the chance of a rollover, although this is unlikely unless a collision occurs. A higher center of gravity also increases body roll when cornering. Increased body roll creates an uncomfortable sensation but is not dangerous.

The goal when lifting a Wrangler JL or Gladiator JT is to use the minimum lift needed for the desired tire size. With a 4-inch lift and aftermarket fenders, 40-inch-tall tires can be used.

Important Lift Considerations

How do you plan to use your Jeep Wrangler JL or Gladiator JT? If you can answer this question before making a purchase, you are ahead of the game. If you have already purchased a rig, answer this question before you begin modifications.

Here are a few options:
• Daily driver
• Overlanding
• Exploring the backcountry
• Rock crawling
• Mall crawling
• All or some of the above

If you plan to do moderate off-roading on easy trails, any level of Wrangler or Gladiator will work. Minimal modifications for a Sport or Sahara would include a tire upgrade to a good all-terrain or mud-terrain tire, a sway-bar disconnect, and rock sliders. Rubicons need no modifications for this level of off-roading. If you want to tackle more difficult terrain, including some moderate rock crawling trails, then the Sport or Sahara models will need a lift to fit larger tires.

The stock Rubicon can run 35-inch-diameter tires due to its taller springs and higher-clearance fenders. Upgrading to 37-inch-diameter tires on the Rubicon requires at least a 2-inch suspension lift. If you plan on overland camping and carrying a lot of gear, including a rooftop tent, consider a little more lift to maintain ground clearance. The extra weight will lower the Jeep, and more lift will compensate for this.

If you plan to build a full-blown rock crawler that can still be a daily driver, starting with a Sport or Sport S makes a lot of sense if you plan to swap all of the features found on the Rubicon. The Rubicon transfer case has a 4.0:1 ratio in 4 low. This is not necessary with the 8-speed automatic transmission. The 2.72:1 low-range ratio in the Sport and Sahara works just fine.

Suspension Travel

Lift kits using taller springs (as opposed to spacers) increase suspension travel. More travel improves traction by allowing the tire contact

Stock Wranglers and Gladiators, especially non-Rubicon versions, have minimal articulation. The stock Wrangler Sport S lifts the left front tire off the ground on the rutted hill climb due to very little articulation. A quick-release front sway-bar disconnect would help. The Rubicon comes with an electric front sway-bar disconnect.

Extreme ruts require extreme axle articulation to maintain tire contact with the ground on all four corners. A 4-inch lift on a Wrangler Sport S shows excellent articulation in extreme conditions. The front sway bar is disconnected to achieve optimum articulation.

patches to remain on the ground over rough terrain. Axle articulation is the ability of the axle to rotate vertically to help keep tires on the ground over rocks, bumps, and ruts. Suspension lifts allow more axle articulation as long as the sway bars are disconnected or aftermarket sway bars are used, such as the RockJock AntiRock sway bars.

The stock Wrangler JL and Gladiator JT brake lines will work with most lift kits, but be cautious. Follow the directions to ensure that the brake lines are out of harm's way and not overextended.

Improved fender-to-tire clearance is an advantage of a body lift. While suspension lifts increase ground clearance under the chassis, including frame-mounted brackets, a body lift does not accomplish this. A body lift is an inexpensive means to gain tire clearance, but it is uncommon.

Lift Kits

Lift kits are available in several different configurations. Which style of lift kit is right for your application? The model of Wrangler or Gladiator

makes a difference. Rubicon models come equipped with taller springs and raised fenders so that larger tires can be fitted stock. Other models require more lift and/or aftermarket fenders to fit larger tires.

An additional consideration is how large of a tire you decide to use, and the tire diameter depends on the desired use for your rig. The more focused you are in knowing your Jeep's desired use, the better the result. The goal is to select a lift height that will accommodate the tire size you choose but lift the Jeep as little as possible. This will keep the center of gravity as low as possible. A lower center of gravity improves stability and reduces the risk of a rollover. This is especially important for overlanding, where rooftop tents and other gear is stowed on a roof rack.

Let's use the choice of 35-inch-diameter tires as an example. If you own a Rubicon Wrangler or Gladiator, you can run 35-inch tires with no modifications. However, if the Jeep is not a Rubicon, a lift and possibly aftermarket fenders to fit 35-inch tires will be needed.

Other variables may require taller lifts. For example, if you plan to overland with several hundred pounds of

Body Lifts

As the name implies, a body lift raises the body from the frame.

Lift Requirements Based on Tire Size and Model		
Tire Size	Non-Rubicon Models	Rubicon Models
33-inch diameter	No lift required	No lift required
35-inch diameter	1.5–2-inch spacer lift	No lift required
37-inch diameter	4-inch lift	2.5-inch lift
39-inch diameter	4-inch lift with aftermarket fenders	4-inch lift
40-inch diameter	4-inch lift with aftermarket fenders	4-inch lift with aftermarket fenders

Body spacers provide an inexpensive way to gain clearance for larger tires. The downside to a body lift is that the chassis is not lifted. Rough Country offers a body spacer kit for the Wrangler JL.

gear, then more lift (or stiffer suspension springs) will be needed to compensate for the additional weight.

Tire Size

The first obstacle in selecting tire size is understanding how the Jeep will be used. This decision can be difficult for two conflicting reasons. First, most newcomers do not understand how capable a stock Jeep Wrangler JL or Gladiator JT actually is. Almost all of the newcomers at the Jeep 4x4 School and on Jeep runs are shocked by the capability of their stock Wrangler JL or Gladiator JT.

The second issue comes into play for many of our clients after an hour or two of off-roading. We ask our students how they intend to use their Jeep. Many underestimate how they will wheel. Many students state that they want to explore easy-to-moderate trails to use their Jeeps to access hiking spots but really have no intention to go rock crawling—that is, until they are exposed to rock crawling.

We recently trained a client who used his stock Jeep Rubicon to access trailheads for ascents to peaks and to set up remote ham radio locations. He had no interest in rock crawling. However, he wanted to push the envelope to try moderate rock crawling since he had experienced situations where he turned around because he was uncertain that he could make it through a rocky section of trail.

He showed us a photo of a rocky section where he decided to turn back. It looked similar to a section of trail called the Little John Bull, which is part of the famed John Bull Trail, a black diamond and Jeep Badge of Honor trail in Big Bear Lake.

A 2-inch spacer lift allows the Gladiator Rubicon to run 37-inch tires. The extra clearance and traction of the taller tires makes tackling a black-diamond Jeep Badge of Honor trail much easier.

This section of trail is relatively easy for a black-diamond route, but it is still challenging. He handled the trail with relative ease. After finishing the run, his first question was, can I handle the rest of the John Bull Trail (which is much more difficult) with 35-inch-diameter tires. Well, yes!

The bottom line is that a suspension lift allows larger tires that allow for improved ground clearance. The desired tire diameter and the model of the Wrangler JL or Gladiator JT are key factors when selecting a lift kit. We will cover the optimum tire sizes for various types of off-roading in Chapter 7.

Spacer Lifts

A spacer lift is an economical way to lift a Wrangler JL or Gladiator JT. Spacer lift kits are inexpensive and available from many manufacturers. Spacer lifts, as the name suggests, use spacers between the stock springs and the body attachment points to lift the vehicle from 0.75 to 2.5 inches.

Spacers can be steel or hard rubber. The stock spring isolators are retained to reduce noise and harshness. Some kits include new bump stops. Shock-absorber extensions may also be included so that the stock shocks can be retained.

A few spring spacer lift kits include beefier lower control arms for added strength and reliability. Spring spacer lifts generally cost less than $500. If shocks are included, the cost will be higher.

While spring spacer lifts increase ground clearance and allow for the fitment of taller tires for more ground clearance, they do not increase suspension travel or articulation because travel is limited by the length of the shorter stock springs. The lack of increased travel becomes an issue in extreme situations with large bumps, deep ruts, and big rocks, where more axle articulation is desirable. Aligning the suspension after installing any lift kit is mandatory to ensure good handling and steering performance and reduce accelerated tire wear.

Several aftermarket companies offer spring spacer lifts: Superlift, Daystar, Rough Country, Rubicon Express, American Expedition Vehicles, Fabtech, Pro Comp, Teraflex, and Zone Off-Road.

Spring Lift Kits

A spring lift kit uses taller springs to lift the vehicle. Springs are the most common and most effective method to raise a Jeep Wrangler or Gladiator. Most companies opt to keep the spring rates very close to the stock factory spring rates to maintain factory ride quality while lifting the vehicle. This presents some design challenges.

Several factors determine the rate of a spring. The wire diameter of the coil spring material is the biggest factor. Other factors include the diameter of the spring and the number of coils in the spring. The left and right front springs on the JL and JT require different springs, which complicates the design process even more. In addition, the springs have a slight bow to provide adequate clearance. Careful adherence to installation instructions is critical.

Springs can also be made in linear-rate, progressive-rate, and dual-rate designs. Linear rate springs are very common, less expensive to manufacture, and easier to design. A linear rate spring features coils that are equally spaced over the entire length of the spring.

A dual-rate spring uses a coil spacing that is closer together in the top portion of the spring and farther apart in the majority of the spring length. When coils are closer together, the spring rate is softer, but suspension travel is reduced. A dual-rate spring allows the softer coils to compress before those with more (stiffer) spacing. The compression of the softer part of spring provides an initial softer, more comfortable ride.

As the softer coils begin to bind, the stiffer coils come into play and the spring rate increases as the spring compresses more. This improves suspension control over harsher terrain. Progressive-rate springs use a design where the distance over the length of the spring constantly increases. Progressive-rate springs incur additional manufacturing costs and offer few benefits over dual-rate springs.

Most coilover springs use two spring elements per corner. Coilovers are true dual-rate springs. Calculating the spring rate requires a more complicated calculation.

The formula for finding combined spring rate is:

$$CR = (R1 * R2) \div (R1 + R2)$$

CR = Combined spring rate
R1 = Spring rate of top spring
R2 = Spring rate of bottom spring (and total spring rate after the stop)

Suspension Geometry

Suspension geometry plays a major role in vehicle drivability and tire wear. Adjustable track bars and upper and lower control arms

The Superlift 4-inch lift for the Wrangler JL is a straightforward installation. Basic hand tools, good mechanical skills, and several hours is all that is needed to complete an installation even in the driveway. A helper is needed.

The MetalCloak Game Changer 3.5-inch lift for the JL includes springs, shocks, and all of the hardware needed for the installation. The MetalCloak lift provides good tire control off-road with excellent articulation and good highway manners.

allow the axles to be aligned square to the chassis and properly centered on the chassis. Adjustable links also allow the proper setting for front-end caster and rear-axle pinion angles.

Short-Arm Lifts

A short-arm lift uses suspension control arms that utilize the stock mounting points on the frame and axles. Some lift kits use the stock suspension control arms, but many replace either the lower control arms or all control arms with heavy-duty links.

The Wrangler JL and Gladiator JT use a four-link suspension in the front and rear to control axle vertical movements. Each suspension link must have at least one end with an adjustable joint to allow suspension alignment. Short-arm lifts are generally the least expensive and by far the easiest to install because no welding or fabrication is necessary.

Companies that manufacture short-arm suspension packages include RockJock by John Currie, Rock Krawler, American Expedition Vehicles (AEV), Superlift, Rubicon Express, Daystar, MetalCloak, Rough Country, FabTech, Teraflex, EVO Manufacturing, Skyjacker, ICON, JKS, Mopar, ProComp, Old Man Emu, and several others.

Long-Arm Lifts

A long-arm lift kit, as the name implies, features longer suspension control arms. A long-arm suspension improves suspension geometry because the axles will swing in a longer arc, which reduces caster change and camber change and improves articulation. Long-arm suspensions require new mounts for the control

arms on the frame. This complicates installation because welding is almost always required. Most companies that manufacture short-arm kits offer long-arm kits as well.

Coilover Lifts

Coilover lifts place the shock absorber inside the coil spring. The shock features a threaded body (or sleeve) that supports the spring. The threads allow the ride height to be adjusted. The advantages to coilovers are improved clearance and the ability to level the vehicle by adjusting spring preload. Coilover suspensions usually require some fabrication for the upper shock mounts on the frame.

Limited shock absorber options are an additional disadvantage. High-end bypass shocks will not work. Most coilover systems use racing shocks. Most coilover setups use two springs mounted in tandem with a spacer in between the springs. Coilovers can improve suspension travel but generally require serious modifications.

Suspension Control Arms

Suspension control arms control the vertical movement of the axles. The stock Wrangler JL and Gladiator JT control arms are not adjustable because the joints are part of the arms and use rubber bushings to provide flexibility. While the stock control arms are perfectly adequate for highway driving and moderate off-roading, they lack the strength for more serious off-road applications. This is especially true for the lower control arms both front and rear. For this reason, many lift kits include at least lower control arms, which are stronger.

The most comprehensive (and expensive) kits replace all of the control arms with stronger arms, which include length adjusters that make it easier to set caster in the front and pinion angle in the rear. Some companies use threaded joints at each end of the control arm to allow length adjustments without having to detach the arm from the mounting bracket.

The MetalCloak Game Changer 3.5-inch lift includes all eight suspension control arms and front and rear track bars. The arm ends feature Duroflex joints that allow considerable motion and great articulation.

RockJock by John Currie makes a 4-inch lift kit for both the Gladiator JT and Wrangler JL. The RockJock front suspension installation is nearly complete. John Currie has won multiple rock-crawling championships and several class wins at the King of the Hammers. His years of experience shows in the exceptional performance of the RockJock suspension off-road. The RockJock suspension also performs well on road.

Track Bars

Track bars locate the front and rear axles laterally in the chassis. One end of the track bar attaches to the frame, and the other end attaches to the axle housing on the opposite side. The stock front and rear track bars are not adjustable. Most aftermarket track bars have adjustments for length to facilitate centering the axle housing with the chassis. Many lift kits include a track bar with adjusters.

When a lift kit is installed, the frame end of the track bar is raised relative to the axle end of the bar. This pulls the axle housing toward the frame side. Aftermarket track bars are longer to compensate for this. Most have adjustable joints to facilitate fine-tuning for optimum alignment.

If the front and rear axles are offset from center, even if they are perfectly square in the chassis, the vehicle will track with the body slightly angled to the direction of travel. The rear tire tracks will be offset from the front tire tracks. This can negatively affect handling and increase aerodynamic drag. Aero drag hurts fuel economy.

Track Bar Relocation Brackets

When installing a suspension lift, the geometry of the track bar changes. For this reason, several companies make track bar relocation brackets. The relocation brackets bring the track-bar geometry close to the original track-bar angle.

If the track bar is not repositioned, the vertical movement of the suspension will cause more lateral (side to side) movement of the axle assembly. This can affect handling on rough surfaces. Track bar relocation brackets are available for both front and rear track bars. Synergy makes a front track bar relocation bracket that also supports the sector shaft in the stock aluminum steering box.

Suspension Control Arm and Track Bar Joints

Suspension joints allow the control arms to pivot for unencumbered vertical movement. The joints also allow some degree of misalignment by allowing the joint to rotate slightly in a lateral plane. This is important when one control arm is

The RockJock rear track bar for the JL uses a Johnny Joint rod end on the frame end of the bar to allow for easy adjustment.

Adjustable control arms allow the axle housing to be adjusted so that it sits squarely in the chassis. Misalignment of the axle causes tire scrub and possible steering issues. Rough Country makes adjustable suspension control arms for the front suspension.

The rotational flex that is built into the MetalCloak Duro-Flex suspension joints allows it to articulate easily to full travel of the suspension. The DuroFlex joints also wear very well.

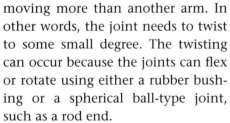

The Johnny Joint from RockJock by John Currie provides extreme angular rotation. The ability to rotate fully improves flex in the suspension and maximizes axle articulation.

Several companies make ball-and-socket suspension joints that offer superior articulation. RockJock Johnny Joints, Rock Krawler Krawler Joints, and Metal-Cloak Duroflex Joints are a few that are available.

Axle Articulation

Good axle articulation improves off-road handling over uneven surfaces. Extreme surfaces, such as large ruts, bumps, and rocks, require good articulation. Free rotational movement of the front and rear axles allows the tire contact patches to stay on the road or trail surface over uneven terrain. This improves traction, helps stabilize the vehicle, and reduces the heart rates of drivers and passengers.

Without good articulation, tires can lift off the ground in moderate-to-extreme rock-crawling situations and terrain with large ruts and bumps. It is important to keep the tire contact patches on the ground as long as possible, even if the

moving more than another arm. In other words, the joint needs to twist to some small degree. The twisting can occur because the joints can flex or rotate using either a rubber bushing or a spherical ball-type joint, such as a rod end.

The Wrangler JL and Gladiator JT feature rubber bushings in the suspension control arms and track bars. Less expensive lift kits that include control arms also often use rubber bushings. Rubber bushings work reasonably well with stock suspension or small lift heights. They do not work well in extreme applications. Rubber bushings help isolate road vibration

and noise but wear more quickly in extreme off-road situations.

Rubber bushings do not wear well when they are flexed to the limits of rotational travel. The rubber begins to break down and cause the bushings to become sloppy, which can be a contributing factor to steering issues, such as shimmy.

Metal joints using a ball-and-socket design last longer and rotate more freely. Rubber bushings will affect axle articulation by limiting or resisting axle rotation. Many premium lift kits feature control arms using rod end– or ball joint–style adjustable ends.

The Gladiator Rubicon shows good articulation on a rocky trail. The Gladiator is equipped with a 2-inch spacer lift from Daystar.

The Superlift 4-inch lift is at full extension or rebound travel on the driver-side front. Even easy roads can have big bumps and ruts. Full flex requires that the front sway bar be disconnected.

The load on the tire is small, so it is not providing much traction. If the tire lifts off the ground, damage to the suspension can occur if the wheel and tire slam back with much force.

Big ruts and bumps place a premium on good axle articulation. Good axle flex helps keep the tires on the road surface, which improves both traction and stability. The Superlift 4-inch JL suspension with King Shocks shows great articulation in a difficult spot.

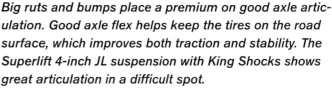

The RockJock 4-inch suspension lift is at full compression or bump travel. The dual-rate spring is compressed at the bottom. The RockJock AntiRock sway bars are designed to allow full axle flex without being disconnected.

The RockJock 4-inch suspension lift is at full rebound, or extension travel. Full-rebound travel helps keep the unweighted tire on the ground.

load is minimal on one tire. When the tire lifts off the ground, it must return at some point. Often, the tire will return to earth harshly, which can damage the suspension and create a situation with reduced stability.

Increased suspension travel and less resistance to body roll will improve axle articulation. Suspension lifts with proper spring rates improve articulation. Sway bars limit articulation, which is why front

When the front sway bar remains connected, wheel travel is limited. Articulation is reduced, and the likelihood of lifting a wheel off the ground increases. When a wheel and tire lift as much as foot or two off the road surface, the Jeep feels very unstable. A rollover is very unlikely, but damage can occur if the raised wheel and tire crash back to the ground.

Extreme rock-crawling trails, including this one at Cougar Buttes near the King of the Hammers course, require full articulation. The RockJock suspension allows the driver-side tire to be stuffed into the fender while the passenger-side front tire is firmly planted on the rocks.

The Gladiator with RockJock's 4-inch lift is flexing nicely. The driver-side suspension still has several inches of bump travel before reaching full flex.

The Gladiator JT and Wrangler JL are both equipped with RockJock 4-inch lift with AntiRock sway bars. Negotiating rocky terrain requires good suspension, shocks, and great articulation.

sway-bar disconnects are important. Disconnecting the front sway bar allows for more suspension travel, which allows for the best axle articulation. The rear sway bar is very light on the Wrangler JLs and Gladiator JTs, so a disconnect is unnecessary.

Sway Bars and Sway-Bar Disconnects

Sway bars control body roll. The sway bars also affect handling balance by controlling where weight transfers while cornering. With-out sway bars on the highway, the amount of body roll would be excessive. Both handling and stability are negatively impacted. Excessive body roll is also uncomfortable for the driver and passengers.

Essentially, sway bars limit

Most lift kits include longer sway-bar links. Very few kits provide quick-disconnect links. If you have a stock, non-Rubicon Wrangler or Gladiator or a lift kit without quick-disconnect front sway-bar links, install the quick-disconnect links on the front bar. Off-road performance and comfort will improve with the front sway bar disconnected.

The Synergy quick-disconnect kit for the front sway bar on the Wrangler JL and Gladiator JT provides a quick and easy way to disconnect the front sway bar when hitting the trail. Reconnecting the bar is also a snap. But be sure that the front wheels are turned straight on level ground to keep the bar from pre-loading. Zero pre-load makes the bar easier to disconnect and connect.

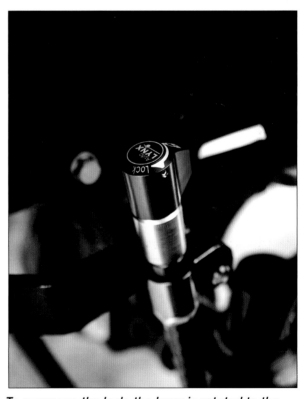

The Apex Designs AutoLYNX sway bar disconnect replaces the stock sway-bar link with a length-adjustable link. Two lengths are available to accommodate 0- to 2.5-inch lifts and another for 3- to 4-inch lifts. When the Apex link is engaged, it works like a solid sway-bar link. The Apex Designs AutoLYNX sway-bar disconnect uses an external tube with an internal shaft that is like a shock absorber. When disengaged, the Apex link slides with virtually zero force, effectively disconnecting the sway bar. When engaged, the sway bar operates normally. A rotating lever is used to unlock and lock the link. To reengage the lock, the lever is rotated to the locked position. One side of the vehicle is bounced for the lock to engage. The opposite side will lock into place when the vehicle is driven. Using the Apex Designs AutoLYNX sway-bar disconnect does not require level ground for engaging or disconnecting the links, which makes this disconnect extremely easy and quick to use.

suspension travel, which is the opposite of what is needed for performance in off-road situations. Sway bars severely limit axle articulation. In addition, sway bars increase ride harshness in the bumpy conditions that are experienced off-road.

Rubicon models are equipped with a front electric sway-bar disconnect. The sway-bar disconnect in the Rubicon simplifies the disconnecting process. Other models of Wranglers and Gladiators need a sway-bar disconnect in the front.

The first modification we recommend to non-Rubicon owners is

a front sway-bar disconnect. Several companies offer them. Prices vary but are reasonable, and a front sway-bar disconnect offers more bang for the buck than just about any performance modification. Sway-bar disconnects are available from Synergy, EVO Manufacturing, JKS, Rough Country, Skyjacker, ICON, and Rancho.

Off-Road Sway Bars

Sway-bar disconnects improve axle articulation significantly. However, a disconnected front sway bar changes the dynamic loading on the rear tires, which affects handling and articulation slightly. The RockJock by John Currie AntiRock Off-Road Sway Bars are engineered to optimize loading on all four tires. This helps equalize tire loads to improve traction in extreme articulation situations.

Balancing tire loads more effectively helps stabilize the vehicle and provides occupants with a more comfortable feeling over the rocks and in deep ruts and big bumps. The body roll on the highway is slightly increased. Drivers quickly adapt to the increased roll angles. A big plus is never having to disconnect the sway bar.

Suspension Alignment

Suspension alignment is critical on all Jeeps, but it is especially important on the Wrangler JL and Gladiator JT when lifted. Suspension alignment should be undertaken anytime modifications are made to the suspension or steering. Proper caster and toe settings at the front and pinion angle at the rear should be set. The axles need to align laterally and be centered in the chassis.

The stock front sway-bar links are too short for a lifted suspension. On the stock suspension, the links can be disconnected using the correct wrench. A quick disconnect is much quicker and easier.

The RockJock AntiRock sway bars are designed for proper loading at the front and rear. If only the front bar is disconnected, the loads on all four tires change, which is not ideal. Optimal tire loading when articulating requires some load on both front and rear sway bars. The RockJock AntiRock sway bars do not require disconnecting.

Toe-in on the front tires is necessary on the Wrangler and Gladiator. The amount is very small. Toe-in is present when the front tires are angled so that they point inward toward each other. Toe-out means that the front tires are pointing away from each other.

Caster Angle (positive)

Front

Upper Ball Joint

Lower Ball Joint

Optimum Caster Angle for Jeep Wrangler JL & Gladiator = 4.5 to 5 degrees positive

Caster is the angle of the steering axis. The upper and lower ball joints determine the caster angle. If the upper ball joint trails the lower ball joint, positive caster is present. The Wranglers and Gladiators require from 4.5 to 5 degrees of positive caster for optimum stability and the steering self-centering effect. Positive caster also resists death wobble. The actual amount of caster is dictated by tire size and suspension lift.

TECH TIP

Wrangler JL and Gladiator JT Alignment Specifications

Caster: 4.5 to 5 degrees positive

Toe: 1/16 to 1/8 inch in depending on tire diameter. Taller tires use less toe-in. ∎

Shock Absorbers

Shock absorbers dampen vibrations. Springs absorb shocks. Confusing, isn't it? When a tire encounters a bump, the suspension spring compresses, absorbing the load and softening the impact. In other words, it absorbs the shock. The shock absorber, which is technically called a vibration damper, controls the movements of the spring.

The most important job of a shock is to stop the spring from oscillating when covering uneven terrain. If a shock absorber is dead (no longer working), the spring will continue to bounce up and down until friction internal to the spring stops the oscillation.

For off-road applications, a shock works overtime, especially on rough roads with washboard sections and whoops. A weak shock will allow the tire contact patches to bounce off of the road surface in these conditions.

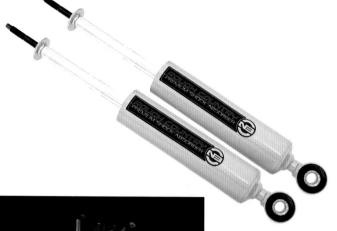

Monotube shocks are the standard for Jeep Wranglers and Gladiators. Twin-tube shocks are nearly nonexistent on Jeeps for off-road use. Monotube shocks come in a wide range of designs and price points. Rough Country makes a very affordable shock that will outperform the stock shocks on non-Rubicon Jeeps.

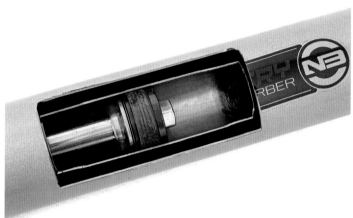

Monotube replacement shocks, such as the Rough Country N3 offer improved performance at a good price over stock replacement shocks.

Monotube shocks use a single tube with a steel shaft and a piston. Bleed valves determine the rate of the shock. Different valving is used for compression and rebound travel.

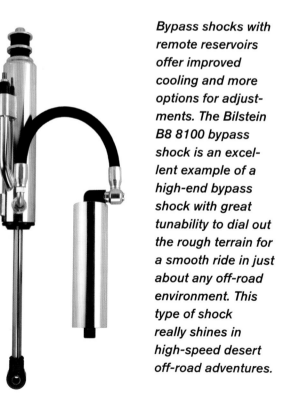

Bypass shocks with remote reservoirs offer improved cooling and more options for adjustments. The Bilstein B8 8100 bypass shock is an excellent example of a high-end bypass shock with great tunability to dial out the rough terrain for a smooth ride in just about any off-road environment. This type of shock really shines in high-speed desert off-road adventures.

MetalCloak offers RockSport JL long-travel shocks. These shocks are available as part of the Game Changer suspension lift or separately.

Boots protect the shaft on the MetalCloak RockSport JL long-travel shocks for the Wrangler JL and Gladiator JT.

If the shock valving is too stiff, the chassis/body will move considerably because the shocks are not absorbing the movement, and the body will move vertically, causing a rough ride and making the vehicle unstable over the bumps. Properly valved and tuned shocks improve traction and ride quality in harsh conditions. Good shocks also allow smooth articulation in the bumps and allow tires to conform to rocks in extreme rock-crawling situations.

Shock absorbers provide damping in both compression and extension travel. Compression is also referred to as bump travel, while extension is often referred to as rebound travel. Valving rates are different for bump and rebound.

The damping force generated by the valving in the shock also varies as the shock absorber shaft speed changes. High-speed situations that are found in the desert or on rough roads cause rapid movements of the suspension. Rock crawling and driving in deep ruts and big bumps causes much slower movement of the suspension, which results in slower shock shaft speeds.

Types of Shocks

Shock absorbers are available in three types: twin tube, monotube, and bypass.

The twin-tube shock is generally found as original equipment or as an OEM replacement shock. Twin-tubes shocks are very inexpensive, but the performance is limited. They tend to overheat easily in bumpy conditions. Overheating reduces the viscosity of the hydraulic oil in the shock, which reduces the ability of the shock to continue functioning properly. Twin-tube shocks wear quickly, especially in the harsh environment of off-roading. They also easily overheat on rough roads and are also prone to breaking the shaft or the welds on the mounting points.

Monotube shocks offer better performance and durability. The valving of a monotube shock allows better control in extreme conditions. Heat dissipation is improved, and monotube shocks are less prone to failure. Most monotube shocks are gas-charged with nitrogen. This helps with damping and heat dissipation. Some higher-end monotube shocks use a valve for the gas, which allows for pressure adjustments that change the damping characteristics for different off-road driving situations.

Shock technology has recently improved significantly with the advent of the bypass shock. This type of shock absorber uses a piston in the shock tube that compresses oil during shock travel. A series of orifices and valves within the piston determine the damping force. On higher-end shocks, these valves can be altered by disassembling the shock or by turning external adjustment screws or knobs. This changes the force produced by the shock. The damping rate of the shock will increase as the speed of the piston shaft increases. All shock absorbers are speed sensitive.

Bypass shocks use a series of valves or openings in the body of the shock, which allows the oil to bypass the piston. These bypasses

The Gladiator Rubicon comes equipped with Fox monotube shocks. The Fox 2.5 internal bypass remote-reservoir shock is a premium shock absorber that is rarely found on a stock vehicle.

King also produces a high-quality shock. The King 2.0 shock offers excellent damping characteristics off-road. The King 3.0 shock does not have remote reservoirs, but for most off-road conditions, it works great. The cost per shock is about $250, and they are worth it.

The Fox Racing remote-reservoir bypass shocks on John Currie's JL are designed for competition (with a price tag to match). They are highly adjustable, which makes them excellent for just about any condition from desert whoops to low-speed rock crawling.

The remoter reservoir on the front Fox Racing shock is mounted remotely due to space limitations, unlike the piggyback-style mount for the rear shocks.

can be adjusted to soften the ride for a variety of off-road conditions. Near the ends of the piston travel in both compression and rebound, oil is forced to flow through the orifices in the piston, which increases the rate of the shock as it nears the limits of travel. This helps keep the shock from bottoming out in harsh road conditions.

Bypass shocks offer external adjustment, usually for both bump and rebound travel. They can be fine-tuned for nearly any condition from low-speed rock crawling to high-speed desert running.

Bypass shocks can be either internal or external. An internal bypass means that the bypasses are

Fox builds high-end shocks for the Wrangler JL and Gladiator JT. These shocks are a step or two below the all-out racing shocks and are priced accordingly. Very few individuals could tell the difference between these versions and full-blown racing shocks.

The rear axle area of the JL (and JT) provides enough room to mount the remote reservoir on the shock body. This piggyback-mounting system is much easier to install. The Bilstein B8 8100 bypass shock offers a really smooth ride at speed in the desert.

maintained within the body of the shock. External bypass shocks have bypass tubes external to the shock body. There is little difference in performance. The one advantage to an internal bypass shock is the compact nature of the shock without external tubes. This allows the internal bypass shock to be used in coilover spring setups.

Remote-reservoir shocks can be either monotube or bypass designs. The remote reservoir can be attached to the shock body or a hose can be used to allow remote mounting locations. The remote mounting allows more options for clearance. The remote reservoir provides a larger quantity of oil that circulates through the shock for improved cooling, and it lowers the possibility of cavitation.

Optimum Shock Valving

Shock absorbers must operate in a wide range of situations. Jeeps in off-road environments place even more demands on shock valving. OEM shocks on the Wrangler JL and Gladiator JT leave something to be desired. At least the Rubicon models have upgraded shocks.

Aftermarket shocks in all categories tend to offer greater durability and better valving. But nonadjustable or rebuildable shocks will be optimum for one type of driving. Off-road performance may or may not be a priority. For this reason, bypass shocks have become very popular, as valving rate adjustments are easily made.

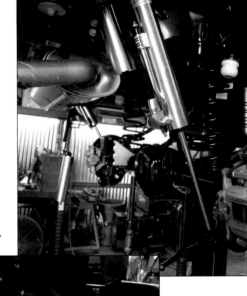

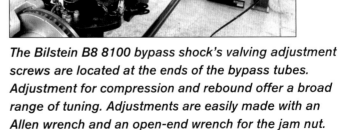

Front shock locations do not offer much room for piggyback-mounted reservoirs. The Bilstein B8 8100 remote reservoir was mounted behind the front bumper. The mounting location is temporary because the reservoir is somewhat exposed to rock damage.

John Currie installs the Bilstein B8 8100 bypass shock on a RockJock-equipped JL Sport S. The B8 shock has adjusting screws for both bump and rebound stiffness. The B8 has a significant range of adjustment.

The Bilstein B8 8100 bypass shock's valving adjustment screws are located at the ends of the bypass tubes. Adjustment for compression and rebound offer a broad range of tuning. Adjustments are easily made with an Allen wrench and an open-end wrench for the jam nut.

Shock Length and Travel

When lifting a Wrangler JL or Gladiator JT, the shock length and travel must be taken into account. Lift kits with shocks often come with shock extension brackets to allow for the lift springs. These brackets allow clearance but not for the additional travel that will allow greater axle articulation. It is best to install a lift kit that includes shocks that are matched to the lift height. Proper-length shocks will allow full travel and articulation and will not hinder the improved performance offered by the lift.

Shaft Diameter

One indication of a shock absorber's durability is the diameter of the shaft. Less expensive aftermarket shocks have shaft diameters in the range of 0.50 to 0.60 inch. Premium shocks have larger shaft diameters up to 7/8 inch. Shafts can bend, and the

Rough Country offers several types of shocks for the Gladiator JT and Wrangler JL. The Vertex shocks feature remote reservoirs on the internal bypass units with eight-stage adjustability.

mounting-end welds are weak points that can break in difficult terrain.

Shock Body Diameter and Piston Area

The diameter of the shock body dictates the piston size and area. The advantage to larger shock bodies and pistons is improved

As with the Bilstein shocks on the Wrangler, the Fox 2.5 bypass remote-reservoir shocks on the front of the Gladiator lack space for a piggyback mount. The Fox Shox use click dials for making adjustments to compression and rebound rates.

cooling and better control of valving. Shock body diameters range from 2 to 3 inches. The most common diameter for most monotube shocks is 2 inches. While larger shocks have some advantages, the 2.90-inch body shocks can offer great off-road performance for a reasonable cost.

Bump Stops and Travel Limit Straps

Shock absorbers can be damaged when they are fully compressed or fully extended, especially if the load is high. Bump stops limit shock travel during compression or bump travel. The bump stop, as the name implies, keeps the shock from bottoming out by limiting travel.

Stock bump stops are made of a hard rubber compound that does

Hydraulic bump stops dampen the impact when a shock reaches the limit of bump, or compression travel. The hydraulic damping creates a smoother ride and reduces the chance of damage to the internals of the shock. The hydraulic bump stops from Rough Country feature threaded bodies so that the height where the bump stop is activated is adjustable.

little to dampen the impact, but the possibility of damage is limited. Many aftermarket lift kits provide taller bump stops to compensate for the increased length of the new shock. These bump stops are made from metal or hard rubber.

Hydraulic bump stops work similarly to a simplified shock absorber to dampen the impact when the bump stop is engaged. Hydraulic bump stops help control axle and wheel movement near the limits of bump travel, but the effect is fairly small compared to the hard-material bump stops. Most bypass shocks have internal bump stops or increased rate valving as the shock nears the extreme of bump travel.

Limiting rebound or extension travel is less critical. The loads are smaller. But limiting rebound travel

When a lift kit is added, bump-stop extensions are needed to limit travel to avoid damage to the shock absorber internals. Most lift kits include bump-stop extensions or new bump stops. Rough Country offers bump-stop extensions separate from a lift kit for both front and rear suspensions.

is necessary when the spring could become unseated from the spring perch due to excessive travel. If the spring unseats, it could fall out of the perch or at a minimum become unseated from the indexed spring perch. Limit straps are made from web material similar to a seat belt. The strap bolts to the chassis at one end and the axle at the other end.

Trail Test No. 1

Vehicle: Jeep Wrangler JLU (four-door)
Modifications: Superlift 4-inch lift kit, King 2.0 shocks

The Superlift 4-inch lift kit is considered to be a budget lift, and the King 2.0 shocks are considered to be premium shock absorbers. The lift kit with shock extension sells for less than $1,000. Adding the King 2.0 shocks raises the price by about $1,000.

The tested kit included the following:
- Location-specific dual-rate coil springs
- Compression-stop spacers (bump stops)
- Extended sway-bar links
- Lower link arms
- Track bar bracket
- King 2.0 monotube gas shocks
- Added clearance for 35- to 37-inch tires
- Hardware
- Comprehensive instructions

We installed the package in a driveway in about six hours (not counting suspension alignment). Two people performed the installation, which included taking time for shooting photos. The installation required basic hand tools, a jack, jack stands, and wheel chocks. The installation was straightforward with no surprises.

The lift easily allows 35-inch tires with stock fenders on a JL Sport model and 37-inch tires on Rubicon models. We fitted aftermarket Rugged Ridge steel-tube fenders with clearance for 37-inch tires on a Sport S.

The extended sway-bar links are important, but they are not quick disconnect. After testing the stock JL Sport S in big ruts, we knew that we needed to have at least the front sway bar disconnected. We disconnected the front sway bar for the test. We went back to the same heavily rutted area and rock-rawling sections where we tested the stock JL. The

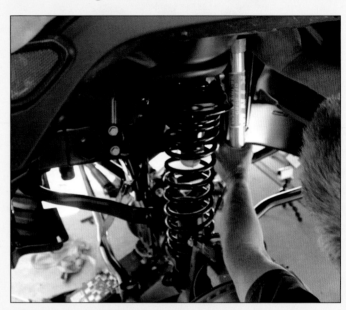

The King 2.0 monotube shocks were nearly the last items to be installed before aligning the suspension.

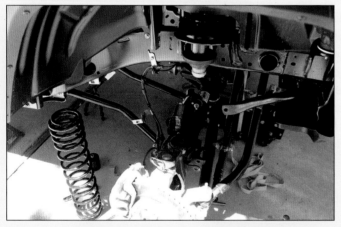

With basic tools, a lift kit can be installed at home. Some experience is helpful, and the job is much easier with two people. We installed the Superlift 4-inch lift kit and King shocks in about six hours. The ratchet strap was used to help align the axle housing laterally when reinstalling the track bar.

The real fun begins when suspension testing takes place. The Superlift springs are a little stiffer than stock but perform well off-road. The King shocks have excellent valving for off-road use and work well on the highway.

The Superlift springs have a very linear feeling. Overall, the compromise is excellent with the Superlift and King shocks package.

most notable capability of the package was on big ruts and bumps. Full articulation kept the tires planted and the vehicle very stable.

On the rocks, tire grip was enhanced by the suspension and the excellent shock valving. The King 2.0 shocks provided great damping in all conditions. One of the drivers loved the ride quality of the suspension while the other driver thought the springs rates were a little too stiff, which added harshness to the ride on bumpy surfaces and washboard sections.

Overall, given the cost and the improvement of off-road capability and tire clearance, this combination of modifications performed beyond expectations and is an excellent package for most off-road conditions.

The Superlift 4-inch lift kit with King shocks flexes extremely well, which is an indication of a well-designed package. The front sway bar is disconnected for off-road driving.

Trail Test No. 2

Vehicle: Jeep Gladiator JT
Modifications: Daystar 2-inch spacer lift (stock Rubicon
springs and shocks)

The 2-inch spacer lift from Daystar provided additional clearance to run up to 37-inch tires. With a price of less than $400, the Daystar lift with stock springs and shocks allows for moderate rock crawling and improved axle articulation. Installation is straightforward.

The Daystar lift included the following:

- Kevlar-infused polyurethane spacers
- Clears 37-inch tires on non-Rubicon models
- Includes front lower control arms, sway-bar end links, extended bump stops, and front shock extensions
- No metal-on-metal contact
- Maintains factory ride quality
- Limited lifetime warranty
- Lift Height: 2 inches
- Location: Front and rear
- Material: Polyurethane

The Daystar lift on the Gladiator has been tested in many types of terrain on both 35- and 37-inch tires. No rubbing or clearance issues occurred, even at full articulation. The suspension works well in ruts, bumps, and rocks. Even extreme trails, such as Hammerdown in Johnson Valley, California, presented no performance problems, although more ground clearance would have been welcomed.

The All J Products Gladiator completed two Jeep Badge of Honor trails (Gold Mountain and Holcomb Creek in Big Bear, California) with minimal issues. Again, more ground clearance would have made rock crawling a little easier.

The stock fenders on the Gladiator Rubicon provide just enough clearance for the 35-inch tires. The 37-inch tires rubbed a little at full articulation. Aftermarket fenders solved the rubbing issue.

The Daystar 2-inch spacer lift with the stock Rubicon springs and the stock Fox shocks is a good all-around combination. The extra ground clearance is necessary for rock-crawling trails, including Gold Mountain, a Jeep Badge of Honor trail in Big Bear.

Before installing the RockJock suspension, we tested the Daystar 2-inch spacer lift kit. On the test, we used 35-inch Nexen Roadian MTX tires and later upgraded to the same tire with a 37-inch diameter. Rubbing was not an issue on the 35-inch tires, but minor rubbing was encountered with the 37-inch tires.

The stock springs with the Daystar spacers allow articulation equal to stock flex with the Rubicon. Taller springs would improve articulation.

Driving narrow notch canyons presents challenges for the Jeep and its driver. Good flex, good traction, and stability are important factors. The JL exceeded expectations.

The Jeep Wrangler JL project rig began life as a Sport S model. The transformation into a full-blown daily driven rock crawler took several months. The JL now has RockJock suspension, Currie 60 Extreme axles, Bilstein B8 8100 bypass shocks, PSC Big Bore power steering, Raceline beadlock wheels, and Mickey Thompson 40-inch Baja Boss tires.

The RockJock suspension provides great flex and just enough clearance for the massive 40-inch Mickey Thompson Baja Boss tires. The Bilstein B8 8100 shocks smooth out the bumps, ruts, whoops, and rocks of Johnson Valley.

Trail Test No. 3

Vehicle: Jeep Wrangler JLU
Modifications: RockJock Pro Edition 4-inch lift kit, Bilstein B8 8100 bypass shocks

Jeep builds very capable off-road vehicles, especially the Wrangler and Gladiator. As good as they are off the showroom floor, there is considerable room for improvement in off-road performance. Suspension upgrades are generally made to allow the fitment of larger tires. Most suspension lift kits accomplish that work fairly well.

For newcomers, it's hard to imagine that a $4,000 lift kit is superior to a $1,000 lift kit, or that a $4,000 set of shocks perform 10 times better than a $400 set of shocks. However, the difference feels huge on the trails, in the rocks, and cruising through the desert whoops.

High-end suspension inspires the confidence to tackle the most difficult terrain. The RockJock by John Currie suspension kit combined with the Bilstein B8 8100 bypass shocks allow the driver to tackle extreme rock-crawling trails aggressively and glide over rough desert terrain quickly while retaining a good, comfortable ride on the highway.

The RockJock and Bilstein combination works! The package exceeded expectations, which were high. The Johnny Joints allow the RockJock control arms to rotate easily for great articulation in extreme ruts, bumps, and rocks. The Bilstein B8 8100 control suspension movements shine over big bumps and whoops. The Bilstein shocks allow the driver to carry more speed with less bouncing. The package provides great performance, but it's the durability that instills confi-

The RockJock suspension and Bilstein shock installation took place on the lift at RockJock. A lift and extra hands made the job much easier.

dence. While the investment is significant, the longevity of the parts helps justify the expenditure.

The RockJock lift kit and Bilstein B8 8100 shocks han-

John Currie helped with the installation of the RockJock suspension.

It took some effort to fit the front Bilstein remote reservoir. The current location is temporary until we can fabricate new mounting brackets to relocate the reservoir to protect it from rock damage.

dled parts of the King of the Hammers route in Johnson Valley and Cougar Buttes, California. Our local black-diamond Jeep Badge of Honor trails presented minimal challenges for the JL equipped with RockJock and Bilstein components.

The complete RockJock Pro Edition suspension lift kit for JL Wrangler Sport/Sahara/Rubicon (without shocks) included:

- 4-inch lift dual-rate front and rear springs
- Urethane front coil spring isolators
- 8 Johnny Joint control arms
- Johnny Joint front and rear track bars
- Front and rear anti-rock sway bar kits
- Front and rear bump stops
- All required hardware

Bilstein B8 8100 Features and Benefits

- The Bump Zone (located above the compression bypass tube) increases bottoming control and eliminates the need for a hydraulic bump stop
- Vehicle-specific tuning with the ability to make a wide range of adjustments

- A bottom-port reservoir hose provides increased bottom-out control during the compression cycle
- Billet rod end with vulcanized mounts for an exact OEM fit and long-term durability
- Dual tube external bypass offers position-sensitive damping with independent adjustment for rebound and compression
- Incremental flow adjuster offers finite and incremental changes in damping force for precise adjustments
- 60-mm large bore hard anodized aluminum piston offers a greater range of damping control and delivers exceptional long-term durability
- 60-mm remote reservoir with machined aluminum chassis mounts
- 18-mm piston rod provides brute tensile strength and reduces internal gas force ramp-up, which provides a smoother ride
- Direct fit for easy installation
- Owner rebuildable ■

Trail Test No. 4

Vehicle: Jeep Gladiator JT
Modifications: RockJock 4-inch lift, Fox bypass shocks

The stock Gladiator Rubicon comes from the factory with Fox 2.0 monotube shocks. The shocks are among the best available on a showroom-stock Jeep or truck. Fox has a great reputation with many successes in off-road racing. Stepping up from the 2.0 monotube Fox to the 2.5 remote-reservoir bypass Fox shock is logical. However, is the upgrade worth the investment of nearly $3,000? On paper, it does not look to be a good expenditure.

Once you drive in rough terrain with the Fox 2.5 remote-reservoir shocks, especially with the RockJock 4-inch lift, you'll be convinced that it is worth every dollar. The Cougar Buttes area of Johnson Valley is a favorite site to test off-road capabilities. Cougar Buttes is especially good for suspension and shock testing. With a range of rock obstacles ranging from moderate to extreme, plus desert terrain with washboard sections, sand, and whoops all close together, it's a perfect spot to test new upgrades for the Gladiator.

The comparison to the stock Gladiator Rubicon Fox

The RockJock AntiRock sway bars do not need to be disconnected. The front-to-rear balance improves during suspension travel, and there is no need to disconnect the front sway bar. Body roll on the highway increases slightly, but it is barely noticeable.

Trail Test No. 4 *continued*

shocks is, well, not very good. The upgrade to the Fox 2.5 remote-reservoir shock is a significant improvement, especially in the rough and bouncy desert terrain. The shock and suspension allow you to carry more speed and glide rather than bounce over the rough stuff.

The investment in the Fox 2.5 remote-reservoir shocks makes sense if you want the versatility of higher-speed desert driving and rock crawling with good on-highway feel. The Fox 2.5 remote-reservoir shocks are especially good when combined with a suspension lift, such as the RockJock 4-inch lift with the AntiRock sway bars.

On the other hand, if you drive more on the highway and partake in moderate off-road adventures, the stock Rubicon will serve you well. A much less expensive upgrade is the 2-inch spacer lift from Daystar, which we also tested. Other companies also offer spacer lift kits. However, if you like to fly across the desert terrain, the RockJock and Fox 2.5 remote-reservoir shock setup is hard to beat.

RockJock Pro Edition 4-Inch JT Suspension Lift

The complete RockJock Pro Edition suspension lift kit (without shocks) for the Gladiator JT includes:

- 4-inch lift dual-rate front and rear springs
- Urethane front coil spring isolators
- 8 Johnny Joint control arms
- Johnny Joint front and rear track bars
- Front and rear anti-rock sway bar kits
- Front and rear bump stops
- Front brake line relocation brackets
- Extended rear brake hose kit
- Driveshaft carrier bearing drop spacer
- All required hardware ■

The Gladiator Rubicon really comes alive with the RockJock by John Currie 4-inch lift, the RockJock AntiRock sway bars, and the Fox 2.5 Bypass remote-reservoir shocks. (Photo Courtesy Toby Jho)

The RockJock suspension shows great flex while the 37-inch Nexen Roadian MTX mud-terrain tires provide excellent sidewall grip in the rocks. (Photo Courtesy Toby Jho)

Installation of the RockJock suspension and Fox shocks presented no surprises. All J Products owner (and coauthor) Quinn Thomas puts the finishing touches on his Gladiator Rubicon.

The RockJock 4-inch lift suspension and Fox remote-reservoir bypass shocks look the part. The Gladiator runs on the stock Dana 44 axle with Artec Trusses.

The Gladiator flexes on the rocks at full rebound on the passenger-side front. Johnson Valley, the home of King of the Hammers, presents serious challenges for the Gladiator, but it handled the terrain with relative ease. The concerns about the Gladiator's off-road performance have proven to be unfounded. (Photo Courtesy Toby Jho)

Installing and Aligning a Lift-Kit Suspension System by Bill Stephens

When installing a lift kit, or even having someone else install it for you, be aware of certain aspects of alignment that can make a difference in the performance and handling of that suspension system. If the lift kit is installed incorrectly, it can limit the vehicle's ability to ride smoothly on the highway, or it may limit the vehicle's travel, articulation, or flex off-road.

Installation is straightforward, but some difficulties can be encountered. The weight of some of the parts and the tight, cramped areas add to the difficulty. If installation will take place in a driveway, as we did with the Superlift kit, the challenge increases but is achievable.

If the installation is conducted in a garage or on a driveway, be sure that the Jeep is resting on jack stands. The Jeep needs to be raised high enough to allow the shocks to be removed. The axles should be supported with a jack so that the electrical connections and brake lines will not stretch or possibly break.

Disconnect the track bar to drop the axle low enough to remove the old springs and install the longer replacement springs into their correct locations, making sure that the springs are properly positioned in the spring seats. Note that the right front spring on JLs is longer than the left. The springs should be marked left or right.

Before installing the new springs, hold the axle in place

with a floor jack, then remove one of the lower control arms. Adjust the length of the new control arm to match the length of the old one as closely as possible. If the axle has remained stationary, the new control arm should fall into place on the frame and axle mounting brackets. Repeat this with the other lower control arm.

Now, repeat the process with the upper control arms. Only install one of the upper control arms from the frame to the axle. Leave the other upper control arm attached only at the frame for now.

Here's where it gets fun. Perform this on one axle at a time. After replacing the upper and lower control arms on either the front or rear axle, install the springs. Remember the right-front spring is longer than the left front. Some maneuvering may be necessary to fit the longer springs. Make sure to rotate the springs so that they are properly positioned in the spring seats and isolators.

Raise the axle with your jack to attach the shocks. This will hold the axle in place. Reattach the brake-line supports and any other wiring.

Typical tools are needed for alignment: a tape measure and a digital magnetic level for adjusting caster and pinion angles. Large wrenches are needed to tighten the jam nuts after the control arms, track bars, drag link, and tie-rods are adjusted to the correct lengths. A helper to hold the other end

John Currie takes a measurement from the inner rim of the wheel to the frame. The measurement needs to be identical on the left and right sides to ensure that the axle housing is centered in the chassis. Lateral alignment is important for stability and clearance. The lateral alignment can be adjusted with the track bar.

Installing a lift kit in a driveway adds to the challenge. Make sure to take safety precautions and use jack stands. In addition to removing the old springs, control arms, and shocks, make sure that brake lines and wiring for the brake sensors are free and clear.

The Superlift 4-inch lift kit is installed. Next, the shocks are mounted. After all of the electrical connections, lines, and wheels and tires are replaced, the suspension is ready to be realigned.

Once the new springs are in place and centered correctly on the spring isolators, the shocks can be installed. A jack under the axle housing can be used to help line up the shock end eye with the frame mounting bracket.

of the tape measure makes suspension alignment much easier and more accurate.

Measure to determine that the axle is perpendicular to the frame. In other words, it should have the exact same distance from the reference point that you selected on the left and right frame rails to the same spot on the left and right of the axle. Choose either lower control arm to adjust this. Adjust one longer or adjust the other shorter. Now, the axle is straight or "square" in the frame, and you'll run down the road straight. Remember, only one upper control arm is connected at this point.

Once this task is complete for the front and rear axles and

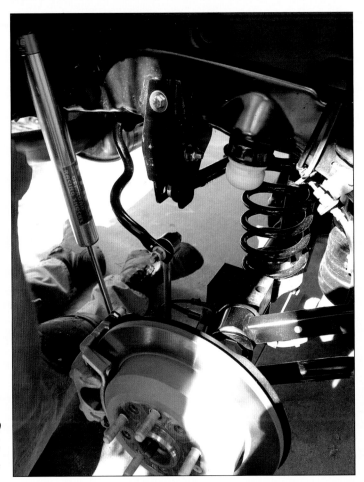

The installation of the Superlift 4-inch lift and King 2.0 shocks is complete. After the wheels and tires are replaced, the suspension alignment can begin.

the wheels and tires have been fitted, set the vehicle on the ground. Next, adjust the new track bar(s) to get the Jeep sitting centered left to right, side to side. Locate identical places on the frame on both sides and measure horizontally to something fixed on the axle or wheel to get the same distance on the left side as the right side. Centering the axle side to side under the frame is the goal.

Once the track bar is set side to side, adjust the caster angle. Caster is the angle of a line passing through the upper and lower ball-joint centers. (See Chapter 4). With a Dana 44 or 30, the preferred negative caster is +4.5 to +5 degrees. (If you're running a Dana 60 or 1-ton axle with 40-inch tires, about +6 to +7.0 is needed.) A magnetic level is needed to measure this angle.

First, set the level on the ground directly below the lower ball joint in the steering spindle near the lower ball joint. Zero the magnetic level on the ground. Place the level on the flat spot at the bottom of the spindle. The difference between the angle from the ground and the angle on the bottom of the spindle is the negative caster angle (top of the spindle is tilted toward the rear of the Jeep).

Ideal caster angles range from +4.5 to +5 degrees, depending on tire size. Adjust the single attached upper control arm to achieve the optimum desired caster angle. Tighten the jam nut(s). Now, adjust the unattached upper control arm to fit the distance to the attachment point on top of the axle. This ensures a neutral position of the axle. The four control arms will not bind as the suspension travels up and down.

The toe-in should not be affected by adjusting the caster angle, but now is a good time to check and adjust toe-in if necessary. With 35- to 37-inch tires, figure somewhere between 1/8- to 3/16-inch toe-in. If you're running 40s on a 1-ton axle, try to get about a 1/16 inch. These measurements are from the tire-tread surface.

The axle must be perpendicular or square in the frame and should sit centered side to side in the frame rails. The caster angle is set for proper steering control and feedback.

Never force the second upper control arm into place by trying to move the axle with clamps, pry bars, or ratchet straps. This will cause the suspension to be in a non-neutral position and will bind as the suspension travels up and down.

Drive the Jeep for several miles then check everything for tightness and play. The Jeep should now track straight, have a least some self-centering effect when the steering is turned, and experience full articulation in the bumps, ruts, and rocks.

Step-by-step review:
- Jack up the Jeep, place jack stands under the frame, and remove the tires.
- Set a jack under the axle you're working on. Make sure the Jeep is high enough so that when the axle is lowered it will drop far enough to get the old springs out and, more importantly, the new longer springs in.
- Remove the shocks, the brake line, and any electrical that won't stretch as the axle is lowered.
- Remove the old springs.
- Remove and replace the lower control arms one at a time, adjusting them as close as you can to the length of the ones you just removed.
- Replace the upper control arms.
- Remember to only attach one upper control arm at this time.
- Install new springs.
- Raise the axle and attach the shocks.
- Attach the brake line supports and the wiring harnesses.
- Adjust the lower control arms to get the axle square to the frame.
- Repeat all this for the other axle.
- Set the Jeep on the ground.
- Adjust the track bars to get the axle the same side to side or "centered" in the frame rails.
- Adjust the upper control arm to get the +4 to +5 degrees positive caster.
- Adjust the remaining upper control arm to fit the distance from the frame to the axle and bolt it in.
- Do a final check to be certain that all has been reattached and torqued.

Shock Tuning the Bilstein B8 8100 Bypass Shock Absorbers

For most Wrangler JL and Gladiator JT owners, a quality monotube shock without adjustments works very well in a wide variety of on- and off-road situations. If you want the ability to tune shocks for a wide variety of terrain, bypass shocks with compression and rebound adjustments provide a wide range of adjustment options for the big bumps in the desert, rough fire roads, rock crawling, and even highway driving. The big drawback is the cost. Companies such as Bilstein, King, Fox, Teraflex Falcon, Rough Country, and Icon offer adjustable shocks, which allows for a wide range of tuning options.

The Bilstein B8 8100 bypass shocks feature bypass tubes for both compression and rebound. The adjustments use 10 full turns of the adjusting screw for a wide range of compression and rebound adjustments. The project Wrangler JL is equipped with the Bilstein B8 8100 bypass shocks. We have tested these shocks in a wide range of terrain and on the highway.

In the JL, the Bilstein shocks provide excellent control on rolling bumps in the desert, which allows for good speed and control to be maintained. In the whoops, no stock-based Jeep Wrangler JL or Gladiator JT will perform like a buggy. The key to a smooth, quick ride through whoops is light weight and suspension travel.

You just cannot get more than about 12 inches of shock travel on a Wrangler JL or Gladiator JT. Buggies typically have shock travel of 20 inches. Low speed in the whoops is needed to avoid damage and maintain something of a comfortable ride. It's just the nature of stock-based Jeep Wrangler JLs and Gladiator JTs.

In the rocks, the Bilstein shocks work extremely well. We wheel on a lot of rough trails with small rocks, small bumps, and ruts. Adjustable shocks can make the ride really comfortable in these conditions. On the highway, our project JL tracks perfectly with a very smooth ride on the less-than-smooth California highways and interstates—even when cruising at 90 mph.

Tuning Guidelines

Every rig and driver will tune shocks a little differently based on feel, the modifications, weight, and desired performance. For optimal performance, adjustable shocks can be tuned for various terrain. For whichever terrain you are tuning, begin setting the shocks in the middle of the adjustment range in both compression and rebound. Then, begin adjusting from there. With Bilsteins, we began five turns from full soft (and also five turns from full stiff) on both compression and rebound on all four corners.

Going stiffer on either compression or rebound slows the movement of the shock. Softer settings allow the shock to move faster. In the desert over rolling bumps where more speed is possible, shock control on the front shocks requires stiffer compression to keep the suspension from bottoming when hitting a bump. Softer rebound on the front will allow

Adjustable shock absorbers, such as the Bilstein B8 8100 bypass shocks, allow fine-tuning for most all on- and off-road conditions. Whoop-de-dos are the exception; Wrangler JLs and Gladiator JTs do not have enough suspension travel and weigh too much for good control in whoops. Low speeds are mandatory. (Photo Courtesy Toby Jho)

the tires to stay planted on the backside of the bump. At the rear, softer compression will allow the rear tires to absorb the impact approaching the bump, while stiffer rebound at the rear will allow the rear tires to stay on the ground leaving the bump.

In the rocks or any articulation situation, stiffer compression will get the downhill tire loaded more quickly. Stiffer rebound allows the uphill tire to move more quickly and maintain contact with the surface more effectively. On the highway, make adjustments for personal ride-comfort preferences.

Higher speeds in the desert on relatively smooth roads and even in rolling bumps can be very comfortable and safe when the shocks are properly tuned. (Photo Courtesy Toby Jho)

The Bilstein B8 8100 bypass shocks feature both compression (bottom) and rebound (top) rate adjustments. The adjusters are easily accessed for quick adjustments.

In the rocks and high-articulation situations, keeping the heavily loaded tire planted firmly is a high priority while allowing the lightly loaded tire to maintain contact the surface. (Photo Courtesy Toby Jho)

STEERING

This is a scenario that could be encountered: You upgraded your Jeep Wrangler JL with a 4-inch lift and 37-inch tires. After a few days, you are driving at 60 mph on the interstate when you hit a big rut in the road. Your Jeep immediately goes into a terrifying "death wobble." Death wobble is very dangerous. The tires were dynamically balanced and your Jeep has only 4,000 miles on the odometer, so no parts should be worn enough to cause death wobble.

On the trails, many situations can strand a Jeep. Aside from a crash, the worst situation involves steering failure. Recovering a vehicle with broken steering is a massive challenge. Forget driving. Towing is difficult. Even if a friend has a trailer, getting a vehicle trailer into extreme terrain situations may not be possible. Broken steering is best to be avoided.

Unfortunately, death wobble (or more likely shimmy) is a common occurrence on the Wrangler JL and Gladiator JT. In 2018, a class-action lawsuit was filed against Fiat Chrysler Automobiles over death wobble issues. The fix was to add a more robust steering damper (stabilizer).

We experienced death wobble on our 2020 JL project rig. We installed a 4-inch lift with 37-inch tires on our Sport S model while retaining the stock axles and steering, including the drag link and tie-rod. We encountered no issues while testing. After we upgraded to Currie 60 Extreme axles and 40-inch tires, we encountered death wobble almost immediately (within a half mile at 25 mph). The JL had less than 1,200 miles at this point. Everything in the axles, including ball joints, was new. The tires were dynamically balanced.

We discovered that the caster

The stock Gladiator JT and Wrangler JL power-steering system lacks performance with larger tires, especially in extreme terrain. The aluminum steering box and electric power-steering pump cannot handle the forces of steering large tires in rock-crawling situations. The steering effort in the rocks can be very heavy, which can make it nearly impossible to steer. (Photo Courtesy Toby Jho)

Aftermarket power-steering systems, such as the PSC Big Bore Wrangler JL and Gladiator JT power-steering system, provide much stronger steering response with little effort from the driver. A power-assist steering ram helps lighten the load on the driver. (Photo Courtesy Toby Jho)

Trails such as Hammer Down in Johnson Valley, California, which is part of the King of the Hammers course, require a strong steering system. This is not a trail where steering issues can be easily addressed. Not only is the stock power-steering system inadequate but also the stock parts are more prone to failure. Steering failures on a challenging trail are not easily addressed. (Photo Courtesy Toby Jho)

angle was too little, which could have caused the death wobble. After adding caster (7 degrees), the death wobble was still present. Most likely, the aluminum steering box was damaged from the first death wobble occurrence. We also learned that death wobble is common on the JL/JT platforms with 37-inch tires and especially on 40-inch tires with stock steering. However, the death wobble seems to occur randomly. It occurs on some vehicles but not on others.

Since the death wobble problem was occurring on stock JL vehicles early on, it is likely linked to the steering box flexing. The early JLs came with aluminum steering boxes as part of the electric steering system. Jeep will replace the aluminum steering box with a stronger cast-iron version.

Newer Wrangler JLs and Gladiator JTs are equipped with the cast-iron steering boxes. The new steering boxes are more rigid, reducing flex of the sector shaft, which seems to solve the wandering problem experienced with the JL/JT models. One of the issues with an aluminum steering box with steel gears and a steel sector shaft stems from the different rates of expansion between the aluminum and the steel. When the steering box heats up, the aluminum box expands more quickly than the steel internal parts.

Free play enters the picture, allowing a sloppy feel to the steering. Over time, this can become more serious. Death wobble can occur in these conditions if a pothole or other rough spot is encountered at the optimum speed and with significant severity. The new steering boxes should also reduce the chance of death wobble until wear within the box becomes an issue. Steering linkage and steering sector shaft breakage is still an issue with lifted JLs and JTs with 37-inch and larger tires. Stay tuned.

How the Steering Works

When the driver turns the steering wheel, the steering shaft rotates gears inside the steering box. The steering gears rotate the sector shaft, which turns the pitman arm, which is outside of the steering box itself. The pitman arm attaches to the drag link with a tie-rod end. The drag link is a bar with adjustable tie-rod ends that allow the steering wheel to be adjusted so that the steering wheel is centered when the wheels are tracking straight ahead.

The drag link runs from the pitman arm on the steering box to the steering knuckle on the opposite side. In the case of the JL and the JT, this is to the right-side knuckle. From the right-side steering knuckle, the tie-rod attaches to the left-side

The PSC power ram assist comes with the PSC Big Bore power-steering system. The ram assist is also available as a stand-alone modification. Using the power ram with the stock JL or Gladiator power steering may cause issues in an already compromised power-steering system.

steering knuckle. While the pitman arm moves the drag link laterally to initiate steering, the tie-rod connects the right side to the left-side steering knuckle to complete the steering movements. The tie-rod also uses tie-rod ends for length adjustments and allows the toe-in settings to be adjusted.

The steering knuckle or unit bearing is supported by upper and lower ball joints that allow the knuckle to pivot for steering. A spindle on the knuckle supports the wheel hub with wheel bearings. The hub attaches to the brake rotor, and wheel studs in the hub hold the wheel and tire in place. All of the components in the steering system will wear, which will cause free play. Free play causes potential steering issues, including slop in the steering wheel, wandering (especially over bumps and ruts on the highway), and even the dreaded death wobble.

Death Wobble

Death wobble (or more commonly shimmy) is felt in the steering wheel as a rapid, often severe shaking of the steering wheel left and right. Death wobble generally occurs when an obstruction in the road, such as a pothole or a severe bump, is encountered. It is more likely to occur while

Death Wobble Causes

- Worn ball joints
- Worn tie-rod ends on the drag link and/or the tie-rod
- Wear or damage to the steering box sector shaft
- Flex or free play in the steering box (more likely with the aluminum steering box)
- Tires out of balance
- Large tires not dynamically balanced
- Alignment, especially too little caster angle
- Wear or damage to track bar rod ends
- Wear or damage to suspension arm bushings or rod ends
- Any steering or suspension link damaged or bent
- Steering or suspension link mounting brackets bent or broken
- Tire pressures too low for higher speeds

steering. Death wobble most often occurs at speeds higher than 40 mph but can happen at lower speeds. While the wobble can be terrifying, it will not cause the vehicle to change direction.

Once initiated, death wobble can be stopped by slowing the vehicle quickly. In some cases, accelerating to a higher speed seems to work, but it is not recommended. The slowing maneuver that is needed to stop death wobble is the dangerous element of death wobble in traffic situations. Steering can still be accomplished while death wobble is present.

The steering system consists of many moving parts that are all subject to wear and possibly extreme loads in challenging off-road scenarios. Wear or slop in any part of the steering system can cause wandering and death wobble. The likelihood of a steering problem increases as the free play increases.

In addition to all of the steering components and links, suspension control arms and track bars have joints where wear can cause issues, but they are less likely to cause death wobble. Additional causes of death wobble include tire balance, tire wear, tire pressure, and alignment.

Steering dampers, also known as steering stabilizers, do not cure death wobble. The steering damper can mask the onset of death wobble but not stop it.

Early Signs

Death wobble due to wear (as opposed to damage) can be felt early on in the steering. When a minor bump or rut is encountered on the highway, the impending death wobble can be felt as a minor shake in the steering wheel. The shake can be very subtle at first but will continually become more noticeable. When the slight shake in the steering wheel is noticed, check for all of the potential causes of death wobble.

Tie-Rods and Drag Links

The tie-rod and drag link are key elements in the steering system. The drag link is a bar with threaded adjustments and rod ends, or joints, for attachment from the steering-box pitman arm to the passenger-side steering knuckle. The tie-rod is a tube with rod ends or joints for attachment to the driver- and passenger-side steering knuckles.

The tie-rod provides an adjustment for setting toe-in. The tie-rod is located in a more vulnerable position in front of the front axle housing, which makes it more susceptible to damage from rocks and other obstacles. The drag link is less vulnerable due to its elevated location. While the drag link and tie-rod on the stock Wrangler JL and Gladiator JT are fairly stout, they are more likely to incur damage from rocks and other severe obstacles. Extreme off-road driving requires more robust tie-rods and drag links to reduce the possibility of bending or breaking on the

The Fox Racing Shox 985-24-173 Performance Series 2.0 Smooth Body IFP steering stabilizer for the 2018–2021 Jeep Wrangler JL and Gladiator JT improves steering feel and reduces wandering, which is common with the aluminum power-steering box. While it is a vast improvement over stock steering stabilizers, no steering stabilizer will eliminate death wobble.

The Fox Racing Shox 985-24-173 Performance Series 2.0 Smooth Body IFP steering stabilizer replaces the stock JL and JT steering stabilizer. Early Wrangler JL steering stabilizers experienced a recall due to complaints concerning wandering on the highway. The Fox steering stabilizer is a much better option over the upgraded stabilizer from Jeep.

The drag link connects the power-steering box pitman arm to the passenger-side steering knuckle. The drag link is a critical element of the steering system. The drag link is used to adjust the steering wheel so that the steering wheel is centered while driving straight ahead. The RockJock drag link is part of the RockJock Currectlync steering system for the Wrangler JL and Gladiator JT. This RockJock drag link is a prototype we tested on a JL. Note the rock rash on the tie-rod.

trail. Heavy-duty steering linkages are available from RockJock (Currect-lync Steering), Synergy, Steer Smarts, and others.

Tie-Rod Ends

Tie-rod ends are used on both tie-rods and drag links. The tie-rod end has a tapered shaft on a pivoting ball, which allows rotational movement as the suspension cycles through vertical and angular travel. An additional shaft at a right angle to the pivoting shaft threads into the tie-rod or drag link tube. Some tie-rods and drag links have only one threaded shaft while the other end is stationary.

The premium drag links and tie-rods use a right-hand thread on one end and a left-hand thread on the opposite end. This allows the shaft to rotate for adjustments without removing the one end of the link from the steering knuckle to facilitate adjustments. RockJock offers heavy-duty tie-rod ends in both left- and right-hand threads. Synergy and Teraflex also offer heavy-duty tie-rod ends. Mopar makes replacement tie-rod ends.

The RockJock tie-rod ends of the Currectlync are much beefier, which makes them better for severe trail use. Strong steering components greatly reduce the risk of parts failure on the trail.

Ball Joints

Each steering knuckle uses an upper and lower ball joint to the knuckle to rotate when steering inputs are applied. Ball joints are exposed to excessive loads when off-road and especially when larger, heavier tires and wheels are used. Worn ball joints are a significant cause of death wobble.

Stock ball joints and original equipment ball joints wear very quickly when they are subjected to the extreme off-road driving situations, such as rock crawling. Aftermarket ball joints handle the heavier

The RockJock Currectlync drag link looks beefier than the stock drag link. The RockJock drag link uses a threaded tube with right- and left-hand threads so that when the jam nuts are loosened, the tube can be rotated either direction to easily facilitate centering the steering wheel.

Dynatrac manufactures really strong replacement ball joints. The Dynatrac ball joints have exceptional wear qualities, and they are fully rebuildable, which increases the life expectancy of the costly product.

loads of off-roading with reduced wear and better strength. Some aftermarket ball joints can be rebuilt. Teraflex, Synergy, and Dynatrac make heavy-duty Wrangler JL and Gladiator JT ball joints.

Steering Dampers

Steering dampers (also called steering stabilizers) act as a horizontal shock absorber to dampen vibrations of the steering system. Steering dampers will reduce steering wander and mask early signs of death wobble. Steering stabilizers provide equal resistance in both directions and are designed to operate in the horizontal plane. Some inexpensive steering dampers are shock absorbers modified to work horizontally.

Some of these dampers use a gas charge, which means they provide different damping forces when moving left compared to moving right. This type of steering damper should be avoided. Stiffer valving in a steering damper increases steering-wheel effort but also provides better feel and reduces wandering. Dual steering dampers also provide these characteristics. Many companies offer steering dampers.

Stock Steering Box and Pump

The stock Wrangler JL and Gladiator JT aluminum steering boxes and

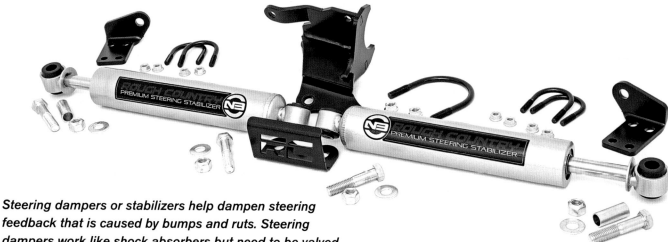

Steering dampers or stabilizers help dampen steering feedback that is caused by bumps and ruts. Steering dampers work like shock absorbers but need to be valved for the same damping force in both directions, unlike a standard suspension shock absorber.

The Rough Country dual steering stabilizer offers good damping from road shock loads. Not only does the dual stabilizer setup add damping force but the dual dampers also ensure equal operation when turning left and right.

The stock Wrangler JL and Gladiator JT steering damper is relatively weak compared to most aftermarket dampers. The stock unit is also prone to rapid wear.

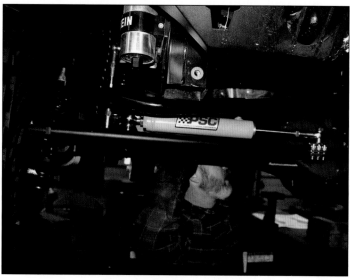

electric power steering pumps leave a lot to be desired. We outlined the deficiencies of the aluminum steering box earlier. The electric power steering pump provides enough pressure for most highway driving situations, but it is not powerful enough for more severe off-road situations (at least with 37-inch and larger tires).

The stock power steering pump does not provide enough pressure to allow steering in tight rock-crawling situations without great effort from the driver. This situation causes consider-

The PSC steering damper is a ram-assist unit that uses hydraulic pressure to dampen steering vibrations and reduce steering effort.

able heat buildup in the power steering fluid. The higher heat in the aluminum steering box accelerates wear, and the disparity in metal expansion

rates creates a sloppy feel in the steering. The 2020-and-newer Wrangler and Gladiator models are equipped with a cast-iron steering box.

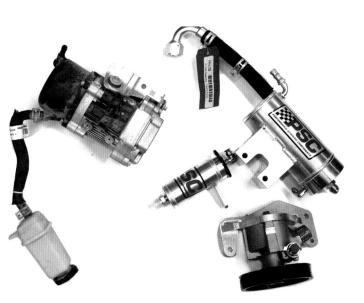

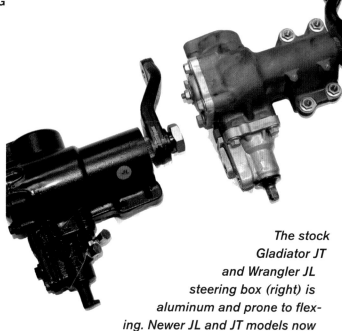

The stock Wrangler JL and Gladiator JT power-steering pump is on the left. The stock pump is electric and does not require a pulley running from the serpentine belt. The power-steering fluid reservoir is plastic. The PSC power-steering pump is mechanical and driven by a pulley from a serpentine belt that is supplied with the kit. The reservoirs are more robust and made from aluminum. The PSC pump is more durable and can put out higher power and fluid volume.

The stock Gladiator JT and Wrangler JL steering box (right) is aluminum and prone to flexing. Newer JL and JT models now use a cast-iron steering box, which should be a significant improvement. The PSC steering box (left) is made from cast iron and has much stronger internal gears and a much stronger sector shaft. The stock aluminum box weighs 22.5 pounds. The PSC steering box weighs a hefty 51 pounds. The weight difference is a clear indication of the durability and performance advantages from the PSC Big Bore power-steering system.

Mopar offers a cast-iron replacement box. We suspect that even the cast-iron steering box will wear excessively under extreme conditions. Similar to the JK models, it is likely that the sector shaft is a weak link and prone to wear and breakage. In addition, a broken sector shaft is a bad thing, especially on a tough trail. If you plan to run taller tires in rocky, rough terrain, upgrade the entire steering system to an aftermarket system, such as the one from PSC Steering.

Power Steering Upgrades

An upgrade to an aftermarket power-steering system provides greatly improved steering performance, much stronger components, and increased reliability. Currently, only PSC Steering offers power-steering kits and hydraulic-ram assists for the Wrangler JL and Gladiator JT.

We have used PSC steering systems on several Jeeps with great success. The PSC Big Bore XD power steering package includes:
- Increased steering torque output
- Relieves stress on steering gearbox and frame mounts
- A steering-assist cylinder acts as a dynamic steering stabilizer
- 100-percent bolt-on, no welding required (with factory tie-rod configuration)
- SG689R Big Bore XD-JL Cylinder Assist Steering Gear Box

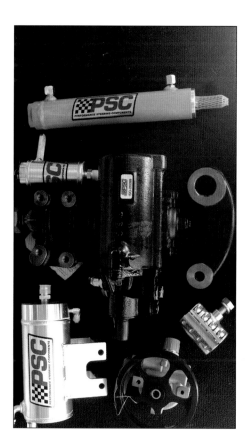

The PSC Big Bore kit includes the big bore, heavy-duty cast-iron steering box, pitman arm, reservoirs, hydraulic ram assist, and a tie-rod mounting bracket for a ram assist cylinder.

- High-flow mechanical pump conversion kit
- Jeep JL reservoir kit
- Upgraded high-pressure hose assembly
- Upgraded return line kit
- Fluid cooler kit
- SC2201K Steering Assist Cylinder Kit
- Tie-rod clamp (available in 1¼, 1³/₈, 1½, 1⁵/₈, and 1¾-inch sizes)
- SWEPCO 715 power-steering fluid

The improvements of the PSC system over the stock power steering in the Wrangler JL and Gladiator JT are significant. They include reduced steering effort, better steering control in tight rock crawling situations, reduced risk of steering failures, and improved reliability.

To see the differences between the stock system and the PSC system, compare the steering boxes. The stock aluminum steering box weighs 22.5 pounds with the pitman arm. The PSC power-steering box weighs 51 pounds. While adding weight has drawbacks, increasing the strength of the power-steering box is well worth the extra weight.

The PSC power-steering system improves maneuverability in tough rock-crawling situations considerably. For rock crawling in extreme conditions and with big 37- to 40-inch tires, the PSC upgrade makes great sense. In the long term, the PSC package will save money and grief.

The PSC Big Bore kit also includes all hardware and fittings, brackets, a new serpentine belt to run the mechanical power-steering pump, and special power-steering fluid.

Power-steering systems operate in extreme conditions off-road. Heat buildup can be extreme. For this reason, PSC also includes a power-steering-fluid cooler in the Big Bore kit. The cooler mounts between the radiator and the grille.

BRAKE UPGRADES

Jeep stepped up its game with the brakes on the Jeep Wrangler JL and Gladiator JT. The latest Jeep Wrangler and Gladiator feature larger brake rotors and upgraded calipers compared to the Wrangler JK.

Stock Brake Performance

When we tested the JK brakes, stopping distances with the stock 33-inch-diameter tires were accept-able. The upgrade to 37-inch-diameter tires caused stopping distances to increase by more than 20 percent. Brake-pedal effort also increased significantly. This was not so with the Wrangler JL and Gladiator JT.

The larger rotors and dual-piston front calipers on the Wrangler JL and Gladiator JT have improved braking performance considerably. We tested the stock brakes with 37-inch tires. While pedal effort is slightly higher for normal stops, the stopping distance with 37-inch-diameter tires is only slightly longer than with the stock 33-inch-diameter tires on the Rubicon models.

While brake upgrades are always a good idea, the Wrangler JL and Gladiator JT do not really need brake upgrades with tires up to a 37-inch diameter. Since 40-inch tires are becoming more common, brake upgrades should be considered and even planned.

Steep descents require good braking performance even with four-wheel-drive low range and first gear. The braking system needs to be capable of controlling downhill speed without excessive pedal pressure for the driver. Brake upgrades help achieve this. (Photo Courtesy Toby Jho)

The stock brakes on the Gladiator JT and Wrangler JL are larger than the brakes on the stock Wrangler JK. The front rotors are vented and have a larger diameter. The Gladiator JT features larger brake rotors, while the Wrangler JL models use different size rotors depending on the model. See the "Stock Brake Specifications" chart for details.

The Gladiator uses large, vented rear rotors and single-piston calipers to ensure optimum performance with heavy loads or when towing.

The stock rear brakes on the Wrangler JL Sport are smaller than on the Rubicon model. Even the smaller brakes on the Sport and Sahara models provide good braking performance with 37-inch-diameter tires.

The Gladiator front brakes use a 12.9-inch vented rotor with a dual-piston caliper. The Gladiator brakes are designed for heavy loads and towing.

The Wrangler JL Sport S and Sahara have smaller brakes than the Rubicon models. The dual-piston calipers and vented front rotors offer good braking performance even on steep descents with 37-inch-diameter tires. Larger tires will strain the stock braking system.

Stock Brake Specifications		
	Wrangler JL	Gladiator JT
Type	Power-assisted, antilock braking system	Power-assisted, antilock braking system
Availability	Standard	—
Front rotor size and type	Sport: 12.9 x 0.94 (330 x 24) vented rotor; Sahara and Rubicon: 12.9 x 1.1 (330 x 28) vented rotor	12.9 x 1.1 (330 x 28) vented rotor
Front caliper size and type	Sport: 1.88 (48) dual-piston floating caliper; Sahara and Rubicon: 2.0 (51) dual-piston floating caliper	2.0 (51) dual-piston floating caliper
Rear rotor size and type	Sport: 12.9 x 0.47 (328 x 12) solid rotor; Sahara and Rubicon: 13.4 x 0.55 (342 x 14) solid rotor	13.6 x 0.86 (345 x 22) vented rotor
Rear caliper size and type	Sport: 1.77 (45) single-piston floating caliper; Sahara and Rubicon: 1.88 (48) single-piston floating caliper	2.0 (51) single-piston floating caliper

Tire Size Effects on Braking Performance

Larger tires weigh more, and much of the additional weight is added to the tire tread. Weight farther from the center of rotation adds to the rotational inertia effect. When weight is rotated, it takes force to begin and cease the rotation. If the weight is closer to the center of rotation, less force is needed to begin the rotation.

If weight is moved away from the center of rotation, it takes more force to move the weight. More force is also needed to slow and stop the rotation. Think of a flywheel. A lightweight, small-diameter flywheel allows an engine to rev quickly and easily. The lightweight flywheel also loses revs very quickly. Replace the lightweight, small flywheel with a heavy, large-diameter one and the

Steep descents tax stock brakes. Larger, heavier tires increase the braking force that is needed to control speed. This requires more pedal effort by the driver and accelerates wear on the brake pads and rotors. Brake system upgrades alleviate this issue.

engine will rev more slowly and also take longer to reduce RPM. Big tires act the same way.

With the Wrangler JK, bigger

Forty-inch-diameter tires weigh considerably more than even a 37-inch tire. Most of the additional weight is on tread rotational inertia. The increased inertia strains the braking system. Consider an upgraded brake kit when running tires that are more than 35 inches in diameter.

brakes were really needed when upgrading to 37-inch-diameter tires. With the Wrangler JL and Gladiator JT, bigger brakes are needed when moving to 40-inch or larger tires.

Large Tires, Pedal Pressure, and Brake Performance

Stopping distances do not increase very much when stepping up to 37-inch tires. Stopping at maximum rates of deceleration (panic stops) does require more brake-pedal pressure. Increasing tire sizes to a 40-inch diameter will affect stopping distances as well, requiring more brake-pedal pressure. Brake rotors and pads will heat more and wear faster. On challenging trails off-road, the negative effects of larger tires is even more pronounced.

Can the brakes apply enough force to control speed when dropping down a steep ledge? The stock Wrangler JL and Gladiator JT brakes cannot stop tire rotation on vertical drop-offs. Even if the front tires do not have adequate traction to avoid lockup on 90-degree or greater drop-offs, the brakes should still be able to lock up the tires on steep drop-offs. Larger-diameter rotors, softer brake pads, and calipers with additional clamping force can all contribute to improved performance.

Brake Rotors

Brake rotors are the heart of the braking system. With clamping force from the brake pads, the rotors reduce the rotation of the wheel and tire. The friction needed to accomplish this important job generates considerable heat. Brake rotors come in two styles: vented and solid.

Vented rotors help dissipate heat for better braking performance in extreme conditions. The Wrangler JL and Gladiator JT come from the factory with larger front vented brake rotors. Both stopping power and

wear are improved over earlier Jeep Wrangler brakes.

A simple way to improve brake performance requires upgrading brake rotors. Mopar offers upgraded heavy-duty rotors as OEM replacements. PowerStop offers several brake-rotor upgrades that range from stock-replacement rotors to extreme duty for off-road and towing.

PowerStop offerings provide options for drilled, slotted, and coated rotors. Drilled and slotted rotors help evacuate the gases that are emitted by the heating of friction material on the brake pads. Coated rotors help dissipate heat and improve wear characteristics.

Brake Calipers

Brake calipers turn hydraulic pressure from the master cylinder through the brake lines into clamping force. The clamping force

squeezes the brake pads against the brake rotor. Brake calipers have pistons internally activated by the brake pedal. The pistons push the pads against the rotors to provide stopping power.

Floating calipers have one or two pistons on one side of the caliper. The other side of the caliper "floats" to squeeze the pads against the rotor. Two piston calipers can generate more clamping force.

Rigid calipers feature pistons on each side of the caliper with two or three pistons per side. Rigid calipers can generate more clamping force. Larger calipers allow the use of larger brake pads. More brake-pad area translates into more braking force for a given pedal pressure.

Stock replacement calipers are available from several companies. Stock replacements will do little to improve stock braking performance. To gain significant braking perfor-

Large dual-piston calipers provide plenty of stopping power for the most extreme off-road conditions. The Ford F350 calipers come as standard equipment on the Currie 60 Extreme front axle assembly. The massive brakes get the job done.

PowerStop offers several brake rotor and brake pad packages. The vented rotors with slots and drilled holes help evacuate gases that are caused from brake-pad chemicals when the brakes get hot. This improves brake-pedal feel and reduces brake fade, which are important characteristics for descending steep hills.

mance improvements, a complete brake kit including rotors, calipers, and brake pads is needed.

Brake Pads

Brake pads consist of a friction material that creates stopping power when it is pressed against the brake rotors by the calipers. Brake pads are available in different hardness compounds. Brake pads need heat to most effectively create stopping friction. Softer compounds generate heat more quickly, while harder compounds take longer to create heat. Harder compounds tend to last longer.

Most OEM brake pads are on the soft side to allow quick heat buildup, especially for emergency-stopping situations. Harder compounds are used in extreme conditions, such as towing heavy loads or driving on curvy mountain roads where hard braking occurs constantly. For off-road driving, while brake performance is critical in extreme rock crawling and steep hill descents, speeds are very low. Maximum braking force is necessary at low speed, requiring a soft brake pad compound. Stock OEM brake pads do well off-road.

While several companies offer replacement brake pads in a variety of compounds, most companies offer brake pad and rotor packages. This way, the rotor materials and the brake-pad compounds are compatible for optimum performance and wear.

Brake Kits

Each element of the braking system must be compatible with the other parts. Upgrading the brake system with a complete kit ensures that the brakes will function as desired. Upgrading to big brakes on the Wran-

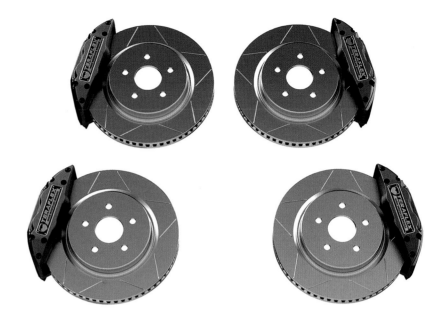

The Teraflex Delta Big Brake kit provides front and rear calipers, rotors, and brake pads. The kit features massive 14-inch-diameter x 1.25-inch-thick vented rotors. The calipers are an opposed four-piston design with 2-inch pistons. The Teraflex Delta brake system is designed to work with the stock proportioning valve and ABS. The Teraflex Delta Big Brake kits are available in both 5-on-5- and 8-on-6.5-inch bolt patterns for 1-ton axles.

gler JK required upgrading the master cylinder and the power booster. For the Wrangler JL and Gladiator JT, most of the brake upgrade kits can use the stock master cylinder and power booster. This not only saves money but also a lot of additional work.

Brake upgrade kits for the Wrangler JL and Gladiator JT are less common than for the Wrangler JK. Alcon and Teraflex offer complete kits, including rotors, calipers, pads, and hardware. Several companies offer rotor and brake pad upgrades that work with the stock calipers. While this minimal upgrade helps improve braking performance, the increase is much less than offered by complete kits.

Kits that include calipers use larger-diameter rotors and larger brake pads. The increased brake-pad surface area provides more stopping power. The calipers in the compete kits generally have more piston area and pro-

vide greater clamping force, which make brake-pedal effort more manageable with larger-diameter tires.

Aftermarket axle assemblies, such as the Currie 60 Extreme axle assemblies for the Wrangler JL and Gladiator JT, come with big brakes. The Currie 60 Extreme front axle features 13-inch vented rotors (more than 1 inch larger than stock) and Ford F350 dual-piston calipers. The Currie 60 Extreme rear axle uses 12-inch-diameter rotors and Jeep JK calipers.

When we installed the Currie 60 Extreme axles on our project JL, we were concerned about compatibility with the stock JL power brakes. The concerns were unfounded. The big brakes on the Currie axles actually performed better with improved brake pedal travel and feel than the stock brakes. In addition, 40-inch-diameter tires were not an issue.

The stock Wrangler JL and Gladiator JT brakes work well on tires up

The Teraflex Delta front caliper looks huge compared to the stock caliper (left). The six-piston caliper provides great clamping force with better force distribution across the brake pad surface. This feature improves performance and reduces wear.

The Currie 60 Extreme front axle assembly comes equipped with large front brake rotors and calipers. The axle hubs use Warn Locking hubs, which do not affect braking performance when unlocked but must be locked for off-road driving in four-wheel drive.

The Ford F350 caliper installed on the Currie 60 Extreme axle assembly is a floating design. A floating caliper means that the dual pistons are on one side of the caliper while the opposite side slides when brake pressure is applied. A rigid caliper, such as the Teraflex and Alcon calipers, has a fixed, ridged design with pistons on opposing sides of the caliper.

Currie uses stock Wrangler JK rear brakes on the Currie 60 Extreme rear axle assembly. The JK rear brakes provide adequate braking capability and offer perfect rear brake balance. The stock master cylinder is retained. The parking brake also comes from the JK but is modified to work in the Wrangler JL and Gladiator JT.

The Gladiator JT Rubicon comes equipped with larger brakes than the Wrangler JL. The Gladiator Rubicon can handle 37-inch-diameter tires with few issues. A brake upgrade using a minimum of aftermarket rotors and brake pads will ensure that the Gladiator can manage steep, rocky descents easily. (Photo Courtesy Toby Jho)

to 35 inches in diameter. The stock brakes are good with 37-inch tires. Going up to 40-inch tires is pushing the limits of the stock brakes. A big brake kit upgrade provides improved performance and should be considered, especially for extreme off-road driving.

Brake Fluid

Brake fluid is hygroscopic, which means that the fluid absorbs water vapor from the air. For this reason, use small pint containers of brake fluid and keep them sealed tightly when not pouring fluid into the master-cylinder reservoir. Water vapor in the fluid will lower its boiling point. This increases compressibility and can cause a spongy brake pedal, even no pedal. Clearly, this can be dangerous. Once contaminated, the brake fluid must be purged from the system and replaced with fresh fluid.

The Department of Transportation (DOT) specifies three common types of brake fluid: DOT 3, DOT 4, and DOT 5. DOT 3 and 4 are the preferred types for high-performance, high-temperature use and are available in a wide range of formulations and performance characteristics. DOT 3 fluids are usually less expensive than DOT 4 fluids and are not as capable in extreme use. DOT 5 is a silicon-based fluid, which is not good for high-temperature use because it expands, becomes compressible, and makes the pedal soft and spongy.

Brake Pad and Rotor Break-In

Courtesy: Wilwood Brakes

After the brake system has been tested and determined safe to operate the vehicle, follow the following steps for the bedding in of all new pad materials. These procedures should only be performed on a racetrack or other location where you can safely and legally obtain speeds up to 65 mph while also being able to rapidly decelerate.

Begin with a series of light decelerations to gradually build some heat in the brakes. Use an on- and off-the-pedal technique by applying the brakes for 3 to 5 seconds. Then, allow them to fully release for a period roughly twice as long as the deceleration cycle. If you use a 5-count during the deceleration interval, use a 10-count during the release to allow the heat to sink into the pads and rotors.

After several cycles of light stops to begin warming the brakes, proceed with a series of medium-to-firm deceleration stops to continue raising the temperature level in the brakes.

Finish the bedding cycle with a series of 8 to 10 hard decelerations from 55 to 65 mph down to 25 mph while allowing a proportionate release and heat-sinking interval between each stop. The pads should now be providing a positive and consistent response.

If any amount of brake fade is observed during the bed-in cycle, immediately begin the cool down cycle.

Drive at a moderate cruising speed with the least amount of brake contact possible until most of the heat has dissipated from the brakes. Avoid sitting stopped with the brake pedal depressed to hold the car in place during this time. Park the vehicle and allow the brakes to cool to ambient air temperature.

Other brake manufacturers use slightly different procedures. It is important to follow the recommended procedures of the manufacturer to optimize brake system performance and life. ∎

DRIVELINES, AXLES, HOUSINGS, DRIVESHAFTS, AND LOCKERS

Gear-ratio questions are among the most often asked online and at our Jeep 4x4 School. Gear-ratio selection must account for several factors. The optimum gear ratio for a given Jeep depends on tire size, transmission and transfer-case gear ratios, and the intended use of the Jeep.

For on-road driving, optimum gearing for highway speeds is in the 2,000- to 2,500-rpm range on level ground. If engine RPM is too low, the engine strains and automatic transmissions downshift to keep the engine speed at optimum levels. Both engine and transmission wear accelerate. Ideally, the engine RPM at, for example, 60 mph with the stock tires and gearing is very close to the same when regearing for larger tires.

For example, take the Wrangler JK Rubicon in fifth (high) gear with a standard 4.1:1 axle ratio, and 32-inch-diameter tires. The engine RPM at highway speeds would be very similar to running 37-inch-diameter tires with a regearing to a 4.88:1 axle ratio. If 37-inch tires were used with the stock 4.10:1 axle ratio, engine RPM would drop below the ideal

RPM for highway cruising. A taller tire acts like having a taller gear ratio.

The ideal gearing for off-road driving depends on the terrain. Very low gear ratios are most necessary for steep (25 degrees or more) descents. Hill climbs with any engine in the Wrangler JL or Gladiator JT lineup has sufficient torque to handle hill climbs and rock crawling with higher gearing.

Descents require gearing to minimize the use of the brakes, especially on long, steep descents. When descending a 25-degree slope, speeds should be kept at or below 3 mph in first-gear low range without needing to use the brakes.

Let's return to the Wrangler JK Rubicon example with the 4.0:1 low-range transfer case gear ratio and 4.88:1 axle ratio. In first-gear

Selecting the ideal gear ratio for the Wrangler JL and Gladiator JT makes a big difference when climbing large rocks and steep hills. (Photo Courtesy Toby Jho)

low range with 37-inch tires, descent speed on a 25-degree slope is about 2 mph without using the brakes or engaging the hill-assist control.

While the criteria for gearing has not changed with the Wrangler JL and Gladiator JT, the transmissions on both the Wrangler JL and Gladiator JT have changed a lot. Both the 6-speed manual and the 8-speed automatic transmissions for the Wrangler JL and Gladiator JT have changed the gearing equation. The extremely low first gear in both transmissions changes how regearing is approached. First-gear acceleration in the stock Wrangler JL and Gladiator JT is brisk.

For example, the first round of modifications on the project Wrangler JL included a 4-inch lift and 37-inch tires. We started with a Wrangler Sport S with a 3.45:1 axle ratio. An axle ratio that high (numerically lower) with 37-inch tires on a JK would kill acceleration.

Comparing a JK with 4.88:1 axle ratio gears on 37-inch tires to the JL with 3.45:1 axle ratios and 37-inch tires was illuminating. The JL with stock gears out-accelerates the JK with 4.88:1 gears easily because of the 8-speed automatic transmission. The manual transmission in the JL has an even lower first-gear ratio. These new factors alter the parameters for gearing choices.

As mentioned earlier, there must be a compromise in gearing for the highway and for off-road driving, unless of course a trail-only rig is planned. On the highway, the first consideration is the final-drive ratio, which determines the speed of the vehicle at a given engine RPM.

A numerically higher ratio means that the vehicle will travel at a slower speed for a given engine RPM with all

Jeep Wrangler JL and Gladiator JT Gear Ratios and Driveline Specifications		
Jeep Wrangler JL and Gladiator JT Gear Ratios	3.6L Automatic Transmission (2018–present)	3.6L Manual Transmission (2018–up) Final Drive ratio—3.45:1 standard, 3.73:1 optional (4.10:1 Rubicon)
1st	4.71	5.13
2nd	3.13	2.63
3rd	2.10	1.53
4th	1.67	1.00
5th	1.28	0.81
6th	1.00	0.72
7th	0.84	—
8th	0.67	—
Reverse	3.53	4.49

Transfer Case Information			
	NV241 COMMAND-TRAC	NV241OR ROCK-TRAC	MP3022 SELEC-TRAC
Available	Standard on Sport and Sahara	Standard on Rubicon	Optional – Sahara
Type	Part-time	Part-time	Full-time
Operating modes	2WD High, 4WD High, Neutral, 4WD Low	2WD High, 4WD High, Neutral, 4WD Low	2WD High, 4WD High, Neutral, 4WD Low
Low-range ratio	2.72:1	4.0:1	2.72:1

Axles	
Front	Dana 30 (Dana 44 on Rubicon models)
Differential type	Open (Dana 30) or Tru-Lok electronic locking (Dana 44)
Axle ratios	3.45, 3.73, 4.10:1
Rear	Dana 35 (Dana 44 on Rubicon models)
Differential type	Open (Sport and Sahara) with available Trac-Lok anti-spin, Tru-Lok electronic locking (Rubicon)
Axle ratios	3.45, 3.73, 4.10:1

The goal for optimum axle gear ratios when tire diameter is increased is to either maintain the same engine RPM for a given highway speed as with the stock vehicle or at least be within about 10 percent of the stock engine RPM for a given highway speed. (Photo Courtesy FCS US LLC)

else being equal. A JL with a 3.45:1 axle ratio and 32-inch-tall tires in eighth gear on the automatic transmission will travel at 78 mph at 2,000 rpm. The Rubicon with the 4.10:1 axle ratio and 33-inch tires will travel at 64 mph at 2,000 rpm. The following chart lists vehicle speeds at 2,000 rpm in eighth gear with the automatic transmission and with various axle ratios and tire sizes:

Axle Gear Ratio	Tire Diameter	Speed at 2,000 rpm
4.88	37 inches	64 mph
4.88	40 inches	69 mph
5.13	37 inches	61 mph
5.13	40 inches	66 mph
5.38	37 inches	58 mph
5.38	40 inches	63 mph

The higher the speed at 2,000 rpm, the less likely the 8-speed automatic transmission will stay or even cruise in eighth gear, especially with the momentum of a larger diameter tire.

The second important criteria relates to off-road performance in low range in the transfer case. The crawl ratio is a measure of the final gear ratio in low range in the transfer case and first gear in the transmission. The crawl ratio is determined by multiplying the axle ratio by the transmission ratio and then multiplying the result by the transfer case ratio.

A Rubicon with an automatic transmission in first gear and low range has a crawl ratio of 77.2:1. The higher the numerical crawl-ratio number, the slower the vehicle speed is at a given engine RPM. The higher number also translates into more torque multiplication, which is important when climbing hills and rock crawling. The higher crawl-ratio number also helps keep speed lower when descending steep hills.

The following table shows OEM and aftermarket axle ratio and transfer-case ratio combinations and the overall crawl ratio. Calculations use the 8-speed ZF 850RE automatic transmission with a 4.71:1 first gear.

OEM and Aftermarket Axle Ratio and Transfer Case Ratio Combinations			
Model	Transfer Case (4LO)	Axle	Crawl Ratio
Rubicon	4.00	4.10	77.2
Unlimited Rubicon	4.00	4.10	77.2
Sahara	2.72	3.45	44.2
Unlimited Sahara	2.72	3.45	44.2
Sport	2.72	3.45	44.2
Unlimited Sport	2.72	3.45	44.2
Optional 3.73:1 final drive ratio	2.72	3.73	47.8
Optional 3.73:1 final drive ratio	4.00	3.73	70.3
Aftermarket rear axle ratio	4.00	4.56	85.9
Aftermarket rear axle ratio	4.00	4.88	91.9
Aftermarket rear axle ratio	4.00	5.13	96.6
Aftermarket rear axle ratio	4.00	5.38	101.4
Aftermarket rear axle ratio	2.72	4.88	62.5
Aftermarket rear axle ratio	2.72	5.13	65.7
Aftermarket rear axle ratio	2.72	5.38	68.9

When increasing tire size for extreme rock crawling, especially when running large tires up to 40-inches in diameter, the axle gear ratios tend to be higher. So, engine RPM will be greater at a given highway speed than stock. Off-road performance is favored when opting for lower (numerically higher) axle ratios. (Photo Courtesy Toby Jho)

The crawl ratio does not take into account the tire diameter. Dividing the crawl ratio by the tire diameter tells a more of a complete story. The following chart shows crawl ratios divided by tire diameter ratios for a variety of axle ratios, tire diameters, and transfer-case ratios.

Crawl Ratio and Tire Diameter			
Axle Ratio	Crawl Ratio	Tire Diameter	Crawl Ration/Tire Diameter Ratio*
With 4.00:1 Transfer Case			
4.56	85.9	35	2.45
4.88	91.9	35	2.62
5.13	96.9	35	2.77
5.38	101.4	35	2.90
4.56	85.9	37	2.32
4.88	91.9	37	2.48
5.13	96.9	37	2.62
5.38	101.4	37	2.74
4.56	85.9	40	2.15
4.88	91.9	40	2.30
5.13	96.9	40	2.42
5.38	101.4	40	2.54
With 2.72:1 Transfer Case			
4.88	62.5	35	1.79
5.13	65.7	35	1.88
5.38	68.9	35	1.97
4.88	62.5	37	1.69
5.13	65.7	37	1.78
5.38	68.9	37	1.86
4.88	62.5	40	1.56
5.13	65.7	40	1.64
5.38	68.9	40	1.73
* Optimum ratio is 1.7 to 2.1:1			

Selecting the optimum axle gear ratio begins with deciding what modifications are planned for the Wrangler JL or Gladiator JT. When modifying a Wrangler JK, the choice of vehicle is pretty simple if even moderate off-roading is planned. The Rubicon model with the 4.0:1 transfer case was the only real choice to get a decent crawl ratio. With the advent of the 8-speed automatic transmission and very low gearing in the manual transmission, the Wrangler JL or Gladiator JT buyer has other options.

With the low gearing in both the automatic and the manual transmission versions, the non-Rubicon models with the 2.72:1 transfer case become viable options, depending on the intended use. The 4.0:1 transfer case in the Rubicon is not necessary to achieve a good crawl ratio if the plan is to change axle assemblies or at least gear ratios.

The 3.45:1 axle ratio that is standard in the Sport and Sahara models

Lower ratio numbers equate to slower speeds at a given engine RPM. Here is a list of vehicle speeds at 700 rpm in first-gear low range with various axle ratios and tire diameters:

Axle Ratio	Tire Diameter	Vehicle Speed
With 4.00:1 Transfer Case		
4.88	37	0.8 mph
4.88	40	0.9 mph
5.13	37	0.76 mph
5.13	40	0.82 mph
5.38	37	0.72 mph
5.38	40	0.78 mph
With 2.72:1 Transfer Case		
4.88	37	1.2 mph
4.88	40	1.3 mph
5.13	37	1.1 mph
5.13	40	1.2 mph
5.38	37	1.1 mph
5.38	40	1.2 mph

Aftermarket axle assemblies, such as the Currie 60 Extreme front axle assembly, offer improved performance, reliability, and durability. Extreme off-road driving, as with rock crawling on extreme trails, puts large loads and extreme stress on the driveline. Heavy-duty axle assemblies are designed to handle the big loads reliably.

is just too high for good off-road performance. If a good off-road-capable Wrangler or Gladiator is wanted without undertaking a major build, then the Rubicon is an excellent choice.

In addition to the 4.0:1 transfer case, front sway-bar disconnect, and electric lockers, the Rubicon offers many other benefits. On the other hand, the Sport S is a nice Jeep, although it is somewhat limited in options. If planning to swap front axle assemblies and an aftermarket lift with a front sway bar disconnect, then you can save $10,000 to $15,000 on the purchase price by selecting the Sport or Sport S over the Rubicon.

When we decided to build rigs for the book project (at least that was our excuse), Quinn went with a Gladiator JT Rubicon and Don selected a Wrangler JL Sport S. At first, Quinn had no

plan to run bigger than 37-inch tires, and he did not want to swap axles. Don planned from the beginning to upgrade axles to Currie 60 Extremes and to run both 37- and 40-inch tires for testing purposes (again, a great excuse).

For Quinn, the choice was simple. He wanted the extra bells and whistles of the Rubicon. He regeared the ring and pinions and added a truss brace to strengthen the front Dana 44 axle housing for improved off-road reliability.

Don's choice was even easier. He planned from the beginning to upgrade the complete axle assemblies to the Currie 60 Extremes with Yukon Gear 5.38:1–ratio ring and pinions and Yukon Zip lockers. The axle lockers on the Rubicon were unnecessary. So was the sway-bar disconnect on the Rubicon. Don chose the RockJock 4-inch lift with the

AntiRock sway bars. The only significant Rubicon feature not changed was the 4.0:1 transfer case.

With the 8-speed automatic transmission, the 4.0:1 low-range transfer case was not needed. The 5.38:1 axle ratio provided a good crawl ratio of nearly 69 and a first-gear low-range idle speed of 1.1 mph with 37-inch tires and 1.2 mph with 40-inch tires.

Regardless of the tire size or axle ratio changes, the computer needs to be reprogrammed to reflect the gear ratio and tire size. Several programmers can be used to recalibrate the computer. The most popular is

Recalibrating the computer to correct for gear ratio changes and tire sizes requires a recalibration tool. Rough Country offers a cost-effective speed recalibration kit for the Wrangler JL and Gladiator JT. Not only will this plug-and-play tool recalibrate the speedometer but it also allows the automatic-transmission shift points to be altered to accommodate larger tires. It can also be used to diagnose check-engine lights and adjust electronic stability control (ESC). The Rough Country Speed Recalibration kit is compatible with all engine versions of the Wrangler JL and Gladiator JT. (Photo Courtesy Rough Country)

Quinn's Gladiator retains the stock Dana 44 axles with Artec trusses and Yukon 5.13:1 ring-and-pinion ratios. The Nexen Roadian MTX tires are 37 inches in diameter. Don's JL features Currie 60 Extreme axles with Yukon Gear 5.38:1 ring-and-pinion ratios. The Mickey Thompson Baja Boss tires are 40 inches in diameter. Both Jeeps work well in the rocks but also have reasonable engine RPM at highway speeds and run easily in eighth gear with the automatic transmission. (Photo Courtesy Toby Jho)

the Tazer from Z Automotive. Rough Country offers a simple programmer to calibrate the speedometer. AEV makes a new version of the ProCal called the Snap. Programmers are covered in more detail in the section in Chapter 11.

Ring and Pinion Gear Upgrades

Ring and pinion swaps are made to maintain optimum engine RPM on the highway and a good crawl ratio off-road. The current transmissions offered on the Wrangler JL and Gladiator JT make the necessity of axle ratio changes a little less critical.

For example, running 35-inch tires on a Rubicon model works well without axle-ratio changes. Various axle housings require different gear designs. The standard axles on the Wrangler JL and Gladiator JT are the Dana 30 front axle and Dana 35 rear axle found on the Sport, Sport S, and other models. The Dana 44 is found on the rear of the Sahara and Rubicon.

Several companies manufacture ring and pinion gears for Wrangler

Yukon Gear & Axle offers a wide range of ring-and-pinion ratios for many Jeep applications. The ring and pinion on the left comes from the stock Dana 44 axle in a Gladiator. The one on the right is a Yukon 5.13:1–ratio replacement ring and pinion gearset. The Yukon gear teeth are much beefier, about 1.5 times thicker at the base.

JL and Gladiator JT models, including Yukon Gear & Axle, Alloy USA, Mopar, Revolution, Motive Gear, G2, and Dana Spicer.

Axle Upgrades

The Jeep Wrangler JL is equipped with three different axle assemblies from the factory. The Sport and Sport S models come with the Dana 30 (M186) front axle and the Dana 35 (M200) rear axle on automatic-transmission models unless they are ordered with the limited-slip differential, which is fitted with the Dana 44. Manual-transmission models are equipped with Dana 44 (M220) axles. The Sahara models are equipped with the Dana 30 front axle and the Dana 44 rear axle.

Stock ring and pinion gears can suffer from premature wear and breakage from extreme off-road activities. The broken tooth on the stock ring gear makes replacement a necessity.

Yellow grease is used to check the proper mating of the ring and pinion gears in a Currie 60 Extreme axle assembly with Yukon ring and pinion gears.

The stock axles from a Wrangler Sport S have a 3.45:1 axle ratio. The front axle is a Dana 30, and the rear axle is a Dana 35. The stock axles and ratio are fine for daily highway driving and easy to moderate off-road trails but lack the strength for rigorous off-roading. The gear ratios are good for tires up to 35 inches off-road but are too high (numerically too low) for highway driving with larger tires.

Rubicon models use the Dana 44 at both front and rear.

All Gladiator JTs are equipped with Dana 44 (M220) axles front and rear. The front Dana 44 axle tubes are 10-mm thicker than the Wrangler JL axle tubes.

Axle shafts are a weak link in the driveline because they can twist or break. The most common cause of axle shaft issues relates to wheelspin. When a driver applies too much throttle in slippery conditions, especially on rocks, wheel spin occurs. The spinning tires heat up, which allows the tires to generate more traction and possibly wear through moisture or loose sand and dirt. A sudden increase in traction can cause an axle shaft to break (or a driveshaft to twist).

Larger tires on stock axles increase the chance of axle breakage. Stock axle shafts are generally made from 1040 or 1541 steel. Aftermarket axles are often made from 4340 Chrome-moly steel and are heat treated. Chrome-moly shafts are much more durable and less prone to breaking.

The Dana 35 rear axle assembly comes stock in the Wrangler Sport and Sport S. For more aggressive off-road driving, the Dana 35 should be replaced with an aftermarket version of the Dana 44 or Dana 60.

Gladiator JT and Wrangler JL models use a front axle disconnect (FAD), which disengages the front axle so that drag from the rotation of the axles and the transfer case is reduced to improve fuel economy. The FAD introduces an additional weak link in the front axle assembly.

Dana Spicer offers a front axle disconnect removal kit for the Wrangler JL and Gladiator JT. A coupler locks the two parts of the right-side axle shaft together. A plate and bolts seal the gap left when the FAD is disconnected.

Front Axle Shafts

The Wrangler JL and Gladiator JT front axle shafts use an axle-disconnect system that keeps the axles from rotating the front driveshaft. This reduces drag and improves fuel economy. The front-axle disconnect (FAD) is a throwback from the Wrangler YJ, which used a vacuum disconnect as opposed to the electric-disconnect system of the Wrangler JL and Gladiator JT.

The axle disconnect becomes another weak link in the system. Several companies offer FAD solutions. Some offer FAD replacement axles, such as RCV Performance. Yukon Gear & Axle offers a replacement axle that eliminates the FAD. Dana Spicer and CAV Fab offer FAD delete plates. The FAD can be disabled with the Tazer programmer. Aftermarket replacement axles for the Dana 30 and Dana 44 front axle assemblies are available from Yukon Gear & Axle, Omix-Ada, Motive Gear, Alloy USA, Dana Spicer, and RCV Performance.

Rear Axle Shafts

Rear axle shafts tend to be more durable than front axle shafts. The rear shafts are a single shaft with no joint to allow steering. Ironically, rear axle shafts tend to break more often than front shafts. Wheelspin on hill climbs and climbing large rocks, as explained earlier, can heat tires, increase traction, and allow the tires to "grab," which sometimes leads to twisting or breakage.

Chrome-moly axle shafts still offer superior strength and reliability. Yukon Gear & Axle, Alloy USA, Omix-Ada, Crown, and Motive Gear offer rear axle shaft upgrades for the Wrangler JL and Gladiator.

Axle Shaft Diameter and Splines

Axle shaft diameter and spline count are indicators of the strength of the axle. Larger-diameter axles with a higher spline count are stronger. The Dana 30 and 35 axle spline count is 27, whereas the Dana 44 front axle uses 30 splines and the Dana 44 rear axle uses 32 splines. Aftermarket axle assemblies, such as the Currie 60 Extreme and the Dynatrac Elite 60, generally feature 35-spline axles, which increases strength and reliability.

Axle Housing Trusses and Braces

Big bumps and ruts are common off-road, and they can catch drivers off-guard. Sliding off big rocks and ledges can cause significant impacts on the axle housings. Extreme trails place considerable stress on axle housings. The new version of the Dana 44 axle housing is stronger than the earlier JK and TJ versions due to axle-tube thickness. The Dana 30 and 35 axle housings are not particularly strong.

All of the stock Wrangler JL and Gladiator JT axle housings are prone to bending. The front axle housing is much more susceptible to

The Artec Industries Apex front axle truss, front lower control-arm skids, and inner C-gussets provide vastly greater strength to the front axle on any Wrangler JL or Gladiator JT. The truss kit is welded into place on a Gladiator Rubicon Dana 44 front axle.

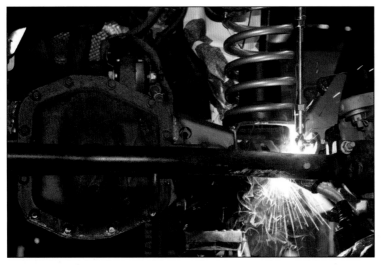

Welding is required to install the Artec Industries Apex Front Axle Truss.

damage than the rear housing, and the larger the tires and more difficult the terrain, the more likely damage will occur. For this reason, several companies offer strengthening solutions to reduce the chance of bending the front axle housing.

Axle housing trusses add considerable strength to the axle housing. The welded truss acts like a span bridge to resist bending loads when the vehicle hits big bumps and ruts or drops off large rocks or ledges. Gussets, brackets, and skidplates are other additions that add strength and durability to stock axle assemblies. Rusty's Off-Road Products, Artec Industries, and EVO Manufacturing offer axle truss kits and other gussets and brackets to strengthen the stock Wrangler JL and Gladiator JT axle housing and mounting brackets.

Full Axle Assembly Swaps

Upgrading to complete axle assemblies solves several problems. Axle housings are stronger, axles are bigger with more spines, big brakes are generally included, brackets are installed for a true bolt-in swap, and lockers and gear ratio options allow complete customization. These

aftermarket housings typically use larger-diameter, thicker-wall axle tubes; heavy-duty brackets with gussets for added strength; and the ability to accommodate a large range of axles and differential lockers. These assemblies are designed as bolt-in replacements for the stock Dana 30, 35, and 44 axle assemblies.

Aftermarket axle assemblies are also designed to retain the factory ESP, ABS, and speedometer sensors as well as the rear parking-brake cables. Currie Enterprises, Dynatrac, G2, and Dana Spicer offer upgraded Dana 44 and Dana 60 axle assemblies.

We upgraded the stock Dana 30 and 35 axle assemblies in our project Wrangler JL Sport S to the Currie 60 Extreme assem-

Currie Enterprises offers the Currie 60 Extreme front axle assembly as a bolt-in replacement on the Gladiator JT and Wrangler JL. At 70 inches wide, the Currie 60 Extreme provides additional tire clearance for wider 13.50 and 14.50 section width tires. The front hubs are Warn Locking Hubs, and the brakes are from a Ford F350 truck. (Photo Courtesy Currie Enterprises)

blies front and rear. Here are some of the specifications from Currie:

- Fully assembled extreme 60 high-pinion front and rear axle assemblies
- 70-inch width provides improved clearance for large tires
- 8-lug wheel bolt pattern for ultimate reliability
- Satin black powder coat finish for long-lasting protection
- High-clearance center section with rotated cover
- High-pinion design raises the driveshaft by 2 inches
- Ring-gear load bolt prevents deflection to deliver maximum high-pinion gear strength
- High-volume, flow-through pinion-oiling system keeps bearings bathed in cool oil
- Rock slider low-friction skidplate, 3½-inch diameter
- 0.375 wall DOM axle tubes, eight-lug (8 x 6.5 inch) with 9/16 studs
- Currie Performance 35-spline (1.5-inch diameter) 4340 chrome-moly inner and outer axle shafts with 1480 U-joint front axles
- Currie Performance double splined, full-floating (35-spline 1.5-inch diameter) 4340 heat-treated chrome-moly rear axles

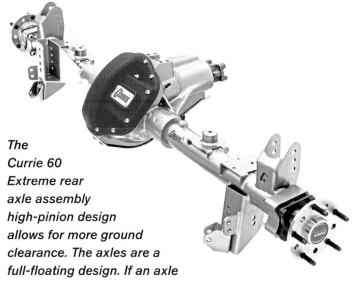

The Currie 60 Extreme rear axle assembly high-pinion design allows for more ground clearance. The axles are a full-floating design. If an axle breaks, the wheel and tire stay in place rather than sliding out of the housing. The brake rotors are 12-inches in diameter and use modified JK calipers. (Photo Courtesy Currie Enterprises)

The Dana 60 derivative axles use larger ring and pinion gears, which provide a more durable and reliable option for extreme off-roading with large tires.

The Currie axle tubes are made from 3-inch-diameter, 0.375-wall drawn-over-mandrel (DOM) tubing.

The Currie 60 Extreme axle assemblies feature a high-pinion design to raise and protect the driveshaft and a differential housing skidplate.

The Currie 60 Extreme front axle uses Currie 1-ton heavy-duty forged-steel inner C end forgings, Currie 1-ton nodular iron steering knuckles machined and keyed for high-steer arms, 1-ton unit bearings with JK tone rings installed for ABS and ESP retention, and Warn Premium locking 35-spline hubs.

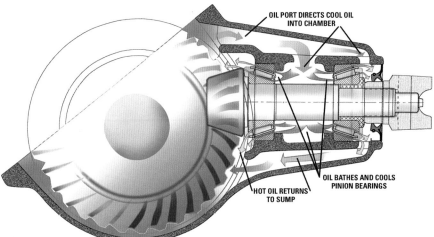

A high-volume recirculating oil system on the Currie 60 Extreme keeps pinion bearings bathed in cool oil, which reduces operating temperatures and eliminates oil starvation issues. (Photo Courtesy Currie Enterprises)

- Integrated raised track bar and ram-assist mount
- Track bar mount height set for 3- to 4-inch lift
- Ram-assist mount setup for PSC 8-inch travel ram
- 8-lug (8 x 6.5 inch) with 9/16 wheel studs

If you own a Sport or Sahara model and want to upgrade to a 4.10:1 gear ratio and differential lockers, an alternative is to use take-offs from upgraded Rubicon models. They are a very cost-effective way to improve performance and reliability. The project Wrangler JL uses Yukon Gear 5.38 ring and pinions and Yukon Zip Lockers in the front and rear. A Yukon compressor activates the lockers.

Selectable Axle Lockers

Differential, or axle, lockers physically lock the left- and right-side axles together so that the axles rotate at the same speed. Differentials are designed so that one wheel on an axle can freewheel. While cornering, the inside tire will rotate slower than the outside tire. The differential allows this to occur without tire scrub.

A differential locker locks the left- and right-side wheels together. This increases traction and also increases tire scrub and steering effort when cornering. Differential lockers are usually associated with extreme four-wheeling situations. However, if you drive in sand, mud, snow, or ice, having at least one differential locker will make life much easier in adverse conditions.

Selectable lockers allow the driver to select when the locker engages by using a switch that activates a solenoid. The solenoid engages the locker with either an electrified magnet or compressed air.

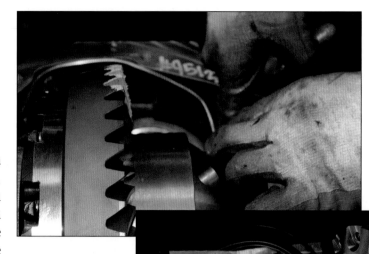

Yukon Gear Zip lockers use copper tubing inside the axle housing for air to the locker.

Yukon Gear & Axle make the Zip air lockers for many applications, including the Currie 60 Extreme axle assemblies.

Rubicon models comes equipped with electric lockers on the front and rear axles. While electric lockers work quite well, they are prone to failure in extreme conditions, often due to electrical issues and actuator failure. Aftermarket electronic lockers tend to be more durable and are a good choice if you are upgrading on models with no lockers.

Air lockers use compressed air from a compressor (or a compressed gas source, such as the carbon dioxide in a Power Tank). Air lockers are more durable and activate more quickly. Aftermarket lockers are also easier to activate than the stock lockers that are found on the Rubicon and some Sahara models.

Limited-Slip Differentials and Detroit Lockers

Limited-slip differentials, such as the Eaton Detroit Truetrac, operate automatically and work well to improve traction. These traction aids are fine for easy-to-moderate off-road driving. Other types of traction aids, including the Detroit locker, are more aggressive, work well in a straight line, but can be difficult to drive in adverse conditions on the highway. For aggressive off-roading, selectable lockers such as electronic lockers or air lockers are preferred.

Driveshafts, Yokes, CV Joints, and U-Joints

When lifting a Wrangler JL or Gladiator JT, stock driveshafts may be too short, depending on the amount of suspension lift. In extreme off-road conditions, the stock JK driveshafts are prone to damage from rocks, twisting, and U-joint failure. The large-diameter rear driveshaft is especially susceptible to damage. Lifted Wrangler JLs and Gladiator JTs also encounter clearance issues with the exhaust pipe.

The solution to these issues is to upgrade the driveshafts to aftermarket products that handle lifts and extreme conditions more effectively. The yokes for the Rubicon models of the Wrangler JL and Gladiator JT vary from the other models due to the transfer-case differences.

Many choices are available for driveshaft upgrades, ranging from 1310 and 1350 U-joint-equipped driveshafts to custom driveshafts for virtually any application. J.E. Reel Drivelines, Tom Wood's, and Adams Driveshaft & Off-Road offer both custom and off-the-shelf driveshafts. Some companies offer only off-the-shelf driveshafts, including Yukon Driveshafts from Randy's Worldwide, Teraflex, MetalCloak and Rough Country.

The Yukon gear air compressor offers a compact solution to operate air lockers very quickly.

JE Reel Drivelines custom builds driveshafts for just about any application. This Wrangler JL front driveshaft was built for the Sport 2.72:1 transfer case to a Currie 60 Extreme front axle assembly.

The stock front driveshaft on the Wrangler JL and Gladiator JT is much stronger than the driveshaft on the Wrangler JK. Note the Jeep grille Easter egg on the driveshaft.

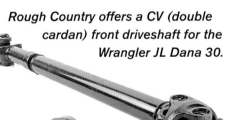

A stock-replacement front driveshaft from Dana Spicer allows more clearance for the exhaust system while increasing driveshaft strength and durability.

Rough Country offers a CV (double cardan) front driveshaft for the Wrangler JL Dana 30.

The custom JE Reel rear driveshaft uses smaller-diameter tubing than stock for improved clearance. The tubing is much heavier than stock, offering greater strength and less chance of damage in the big rocks.

JE Reel driveshafts use a 3110 U-joint on stock replacement shafts and a 3150 U-joint on custom driveshafts.

Regearing a Wrangler JL or Gladiator JT

"Should I regear my Jeep?" is a very common question. Four bits of information are needed to help answer that question:

- What is the current axle gear ratio?
- What is the current tire diameter?
- What is the planned tire size?
- What is the current transfer case low-range gear ratio?

Increasing tire diameter is like using a higher gear ratio (lower numerically). Engine RPM at a given speed will decrease with a taller tire. If the engine RPM drops below the optimum power band, performance and fuel economy will suffer.

With the 8-speed automatic transmission, the transmission will likely not cruise in eighth gear. For example, a Rubicon using the 3.6L Pentastar engine with 4.10:1 gearing will turn 1,679 rpm at 60 mph in eighth gear. If you go to a 37-inch tire (from the stock 33-inch-diameter tire), the 60-mph engine RPM drops to 1,497, which is out of the optimum RPM range. Will the Jeep run with 37-inch tires? Yes, but highway performance will suffer. The engine has plenty of torque to pull the tires, but acceleration will suffer.

Regearing to a 4.56:1 ring-and-pinion ratio gets the RPM close to the stock RPM for a given speed. However, go up at least one ratio (numerically) to help compensate

The ring and pinion gears (left) are from a Gladiator Rubicon with a 4.10:1 ratio. The replacement gears (right) are Yukon Gear & Axle 5.13:1–ratio ring and pinion gears. The Yukon gear teeth are significantly wider and are not cut as deep. The shallower cut means less leverage on the teeth. Combined with the wider tooth base, the Yukon gears are much stronger.

will help when rock crawling or climbing and descending steep hills.

The following chart shows the engine RPM on a Wrangler JL or Gladiator JT with the 3.6L Pentastar engine at 60 mph in eighth gear on the automatic transmission. As a rule of thumb, it is better to go to a lower gear ratio that will increase engine RPM slightly than to have a higher ratio. In the case of having a 2.72:1 low-range transfer case, the lower ratio is even more beneficial for extreme terrain.

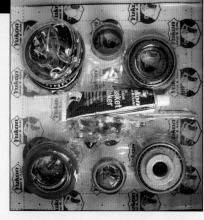

Aligning the teeth of the ring gear to the pinion gear is critical for good wear and reliability.

When regearing, always use an installation kit, such as the one from Yukon Gear. Installation (or rebuild) kits include new bearings, seals, bearing races, gaskets, and hardware.

Regearing Chart						
Note: Tire size, final-drive ratio, and engine RPM are at 60 mph in 8th gear with a JL/JT automatic transmission.						
	Tire Diameter					
Final-Drive Ratio	**33**	**35**	**37**	**38**	**40**	**42**
3.73	1,527	1,440	1,362	1,326	1,260	1,200
4.1	1,679	1,582	1,497	1,458	1,385	1,319
4.56	1,867	1,760	1,665	1,621	1,540	1,467
4.88	1,998	1,884	1,782	1,735	1,648	1,570
5.13	2,101	1,980	1,873	1,824	1,733	1,650
5.38	2,203	2,077	1,965	1,913	1,817	1,730

Once gear ratios have been selected, the installation process can begin. Installing ring-and-pinon gears is tricky. For most people, having a qualified shop do the installation is a good idea. The best scenario is to use an installer with a certification. Yukon Gear & Axle has a Master Installer Certification program that is quite intense. Here are five tips to help even if a shop is doing the installation:

- Select quality gears from a known manufacturer
- Use an installation kit with new bearings, bolts, and other hardware
- Proper meshing of the teeth on the ring gear to the teeth on the pinion gear is critical
- Make sure everything is properly torqued
- Follow the gear manufacturer's recommendations for gear break-in ∎

for the heavier tire and the associated rotational inertia. A 4.88:1 ratio is ideal, or going to a 5.13:1 ratio is good for off-road performance in extreme terrain. The lower ratio (higher numerically) will also improve the crawl ratio, which

OFF-ROAD TIRES AND WHEELS

The following are two of the most common tire questions asked by students and customers:

- What tires do you run?
- To which tires should I upgrade?

Tire upgrades, specifically larger, taller tires, fulfill three objectives for the Jeep owner. Taller tires increase ground clearance, and larger tires increase traction and add an aggressive look to any Wrangler JL or Gladiator JT. Of course, those questions lead us to another series of questions:

- Is it a daily driver or mostly a trail rig?
- In which type of terrain will it be used? (rock crawling, overlanding, etc.)
- Is noise an issue?
- Is tire wear an issue?
- In what conditions do you drive? (mud, snow, ice, rocks, etc.)
- Is the rig lifted? How much?
- Will standard or beadlock wheels be used?
- What size is preferred?
- What axles are being used?

While there are many excellent all-terrain, mud-terrain, and hybrid tires available, significant differences between tires can complicate the decision-making process. The problem relates to tire design and the

Tire traction in the rocks makes the difference between navigating the boulders, getting stuck, or even damaging underside components. Tire compound, tread block design, siping, sidewall stiffness, and tire pressure all contribute to tire traction. (Photo Courtesy Toby Jho)

Steep descents on granite require good tire traction to control speed. The Mickey Thompson Baja Boss 40-inch-diameter mud-terrain tires offer plenty of grip to safely descend steep slopes, such as Chicken Rock in Cougar Buttes, which is part of the Johnson Valley National Off-Highway Vehicle (OHV) area and home of the King of the Hammers event. (Photo Courtesy Toby Jho)

50 PSI

27 PSI

14 PSI

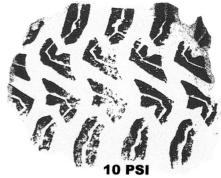

10 PSI

One factor affecting tire traction relates to tire pressure. The Nexen Roadian MTX mud-terrain tire features a fairly flexible sidewall construction. The tire contact patch impressions show the actual tire contact patch area at four different PSI settings. Little difference exists between contact patch areas at 50 psi versus 27 psi. Major increases exist in contact-patch areas at 14 and 10 psi. The larger the contact-patch area, the greater the increase in traction. The contact patch increases by more than double when airing down from 27 to 14 psi. From 27 to 10 psi, the contact-patch area nearly triples.

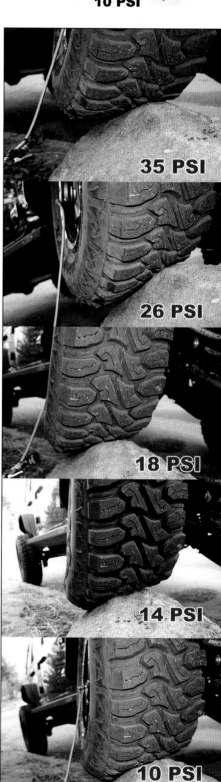

35 PSI

26 PSI

18 PSI

14 PSI

10 PSI

The Falken WildPeak MT01 features a stiff sidewall construction. This tire needs to be aired down more to achieve the same tire contact spread as a softer sidewall tire. The tire pressures shown are 28 psi (top); about 12 psi (middle), which is about the lowest advisable for non-beadlock wheels; and 6 psi (bottom). The tire conforms to the rock much more effectively. This series of photos was taken on a much heavier Jeep. A lighter YJ would need even lower tire pressures for good contact patch compliance.

Tire pressures affect the ability of the tire to wrap around rocks. When a tire can conform to the shape of a rock, traction improves significantly. The Nexen Roadian MTX mud-terrain tire has a flexible sidewall compared with some other tires. The tire pressure shown here varies for different tires. Most tires need a lower pressure to obtain the same amount of tire flex and conformity.

effect of design and construction on performance, both on- and off-road. Most tire-store sales staff and technicians do not have the information in certain areas of design and construction to offer sound advice. Specifically, the areas of tread design and sidewall construction make a difference, but little information is available about either item.

The same questions are very common on social media as well. When the question regarding what tire to run is asked, it is normal for dozens to respond with suggestions, most often the suggestion is the tire the responder is using. Most people love their tires, and rightfully so. Tires require a big investment. Occasionally people relate negative experiences. All of the information can be helpful, but the information is based on limited experience. Even those individuals who have used several brands and types of tires over a period of years offer input that is valid but lacks any direct comparisons.

Tire testing can provide interesting insights into tire performance. The authors are fortunate to have tested many tires over the years. Through the Jeep 4x4 School, we have conducted tire-comparison tests for multiple tire companies. The experience is invaluable. In addition to being fun and challenging, we have gained considerable insight into design parameters that affect off-road performance. Before we get into specifics, let's look at how we perform tire comparison tests.

Tire Testing

Tire testing requires a tremendous amount of effort. We use a single Jeep and swap tires after a single test. Sometimes we group two to three tests together. For example, hill climbs and descents can easily be grouped together. We generally conduct more than 20 different tests over the span of several days.

We test up to five different tires of the same size and type, and each set of tires is mounted on identical wheels. Of course, this requires five wheel-and-tire swaps per test (or group of tests). The tire changes all occur in the field. During the course of a test, we swap four wheels and tires five to six times (up to 240 individual wheel/tire changes). We also test wheel studs and lug nuts as well as electric impact batteries. We have often needed to replace wheel studs and lug nuts midway through a test run.

Here are the tests we conduct:
- Hill climb on packed dirt (45-degree slope)
- Hill descent on packed dirt (45-degree slope)
- Hill climb on loose rock (30-plus-degree slope)
- Hill descent on loose rock (30-plus-degree slope)
- Hill climb on hard rock (45-degree slope)
- Hill descent on hard rock (45-degree slope)
- Extreme ruts
- High-speed handling on dirt roads (up to 55 mph)
- Sidewall traction on a V-notch
- Sidewall traction of large rocks
- Tread traction on large rocks
- Climbing steep ledges
- Descending steep ledges
- Climbing undercut ledges (ledge taller than the tire radius)
- Dirt side slopes (up to 45 degrees)
- High-speed dirt handling (50 to 55 mph)

Tire sidewall design and construction play a major role in providing sidewall traction in extreme terrain. V-notches are tricky, and sidewall traction makes a difference between gripping the side of the near vertical wall or slipping off the wall and damaging the vehicle. (Photo Courtesy Toby Jho)

Hill climbs with big ruts put a premium on tire traction. Airing down the tires increases the tire contact patch or footprint. A larger footprint in these conditions can be the difference between reaching the top of the rutted climb or having to back down.

The stock Wrangler JL Sport S tires are 31 inches in diameter. The small tires have short sidewalls, which limits how much the tire can be aired down. Higher pressures result in a smaller contact patch and reduced traction on a small tire with already-limited traction.

- Highway noise (at 50 mph)
- Asphalt braking performance
- Snow (when possible)
- Ice (when possible)
- Mud (when possible)
- Measure tread hardness
- Measure sidewall stiffness

In all tests except the noise test, we look at traction. We compare traction from one tire to the others. Did the tire make the length of a climb? Was there wheelspin? Were lockers needed? How far did the tire make it up a slope? Was there wheel lockup on a descent? Did the tire slide down a side slope? Did the tire slide off a sloped rock?

Variance between tires is the norm. No one tire outperforms the others in all tests. The least capable tire overall may be the best in one test. The biggest challenge is attempting to duplicate the exact path for each tire on each test. We use spotters and markers to help with this. However, rocks move and ruts can deepen.

We use two drivers on back-to-back test runs. Each driver evaluates the performance inde-

Rock crawling places a premium on tire traction. Tire sidewalls are often the only part of a tire in contact with the rock. The sidewall tread pattern design affects traction. (Photo Courtesy Toby Jho)

Wet and snowy conditions can make climbing rock ledges very difficult. A little wheelspin can burn through the wet surface and heat up the tire tread to increase traction enough to ascend the ledge.

pendently. We also take video of every test both on board the vehicle and outside. This allows additional evaluation. One or two tires emerge as working better than the others overall, but at the end of the day, the differences are fairly small.

Most tires have good-to-excellent traction moving forward when climbing or descending. The biggest differences occur with lateral traction. One tire may hold better on a

A tread depth gauge can be used to measure the thickness of the tire tread. Taller tread blocks can improve traction on very soft surfaces, such as silt and sand. Tread depth measurements also allow for the monitoring of tire wear.

Undercut rocks create a major obstacle to climbing. If the top of the rock is taller than the center of the tire, then the vehicle must either move backward while trying to move forward, which cannot really occur, or the tire must wrap around the rock to allow the vehicle to move forward and climb. At 12 psi, the Nexen Roadian MTX has no problem ascending the undercut rock. However, if this tire was inflated to 35 psi (a normal highway tire pressure), climbing up the rock would be nearly impossible.

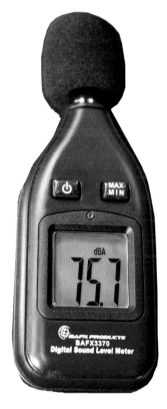

A durometer measures the hardness of rubber compounds. The "Shore A" scale is used for measuring tire tread compounds. A lower durometer reading number indicates a softer tire compound. The hardness range for off-road tires on the Shore A scale is from about 60 to 80. Lower numbers provide more traction, while higher numbers on the scale indicate better wear characteristics. The Shore A scale numbers can change with tire temperatures and with tire age. Hotter temperatures lower the numbers, and age increases hardness.

Tire road noise is a concern for many off-road tire buyers. A decibel (dB) meter can measure road noise. We measure at 45 mph, which is a compromise between tire noise and wind noise. Higher speeds, especially on a Wrangler JL or Gladiator JT, can generate more wind noise than tire noise. At 45 mph, wind noise is minimal, which allows tire noise to dominate.

side slope of a slanted rock. Some sidewalls hold better in a V-notch than others.

Results

At least five factors affect tire traction and noise, especially lateral tire traction on side slopes, V-notch walls, and slanted rocks. Those factors are tread-block shape and size; siping, especially longitudinal siping; sidewall design; tread compound; and sidewall construction.

The tread-block size and shape affect forward traction when climbing and dropping off ledges as well as under braking. Traction is affected by tread blocks, but the difference between tires is relatively small on hard surfaces.

On soft surfaces, such as mud, sand, and snow, the tread-block design makes a difference. Aggressive tread blocks work better in sand. Think of a steamboat paddle wheel. Tread blocks also affect noise. The pattern of siping on the tread blocks makes a bigger difference. When there are more longitudinal sipes (sipes more parallel to the direction of tire rotation), the tire has better lateral grip. The edges of the sipes separate slightly under load and improve lateral traction. Lateral siping affects forward or longitudinal traction. Sidewall design (the shape and size of the sidewall tread) will affect traction when the sidewall is engaged on a wall or the side of rock.

Tire tread compound plays a big role. Softer tires make more grip. Non-street-legal tires called "stickies" are becoming more popular for extreme rock crawling, especially on extreme waterfall obstacles, such as those found at Sand Hollow State Park in Utah and at the Hammers trails in Johnson Valley, California.

Soft tire compounds wear much more quickly. One of the most significant factors is sidewall construction. While tire pressure is a major influence on sidewall flex, the sidewall construction, mostly the angles of the sidewall cords, affect the optimum tire pressure for a given tire. In our testing, we learned that determining the optimum tire pressure of each tire makes a difference in tire traction. The ability of a tire to wrap around an undercut ledge or a rock makes a huge difference in traction and overall performance.

Here's an example: Our team has had extensive experience with the Falken WildPeak M/T and the Nexen Roadian MTX. We'll cover finding the optimum tire pressure for a given tire on a given vehicle later in this chapter. The optimum tire pressure on a JKU running 37-12.50x17 tires was 10 psi on the Falken WildPeak M/Ts and 14 psi on the Nexen Roadian MTX tires, and the difference was almost entirely the sidewall construction.

At the optimum pressures, each tire performed very well with very little difference. However, if the Falken pressure was raised to 14 psi, traction and performance suffered. If the pressure of the Nexen was lowered to 10 psi, sidewall damage was possible if the tire was pinched between the rim and a rock or a rut. Optimizing tire pressure is extremely import for optimum performance.

Off-Road Tire Pressure

Every off-road tire and vehicle combination has an optimum tire-pressure range for off-road driving. The goal when setting tire pressure for off-road driving is to maximize the size of the tire contact patch without lowering the tire pressure so much that tire damage is likely on rough surfaces. Two factors contribute to the optimum tire pressure: sidewall stiffness and vehicle weight on the tire. Flexible tire sidewalls need more pressure at the optimum setting. Heavier vehicles need more pressure at the optimum pressure.

A simple measurement will determine the optimum pressure on a Wrangler JL or Gladiator JT. We learned this procedure several years ago from Harry Llewellyn of Coyote Enterprises (Coyote Deflators), and we have used this on countless tires ever since.

The goal is to find a pressure that expands the tire contact patch on the ground without lowering the pressure so much that the tire bead can come unseated or the bead and sidewall can be damaged if pinched between the wheel rim and a rock or the ground. Harry determined that the sidewall height from the ground to the bottom of the rim is key. He also determined that reducing pressure in the tire from being fully inflated to a measurement that is between 75 and 90 percent of maximum pressure meets the criteria for the optimum tire contact patch and protects the tire from damage. For relatively smooth roads, the 90-percent height works well. For most off-roading in the dry, 85 percent is just about perfect. For soft surfaces such as sand, mud, or snow, between 75 and 80 percent works well.

When we began measuring sidewalls, we inflated to the maximum inflation pressure listed on the tire sidewall. We quickly learned that there is virtually no difference between maximum inflation pressure, up to 80 psi on some tires, and an inflation pressure of about 40 to 50 psi. We use 40 psi as a starting point and measure the tire sidewall height from the ground to the bottom of the wheel rim.

For most off-road situations, we deflate the tire until the measurement is 85 percent of the maximum inflation pressure. For sand or snow, we drop down to around 75 percent or slightly taller.

For example, a 37-inch tire on a 17-inch-diameter rim has a fully inflated sidewall height of 10 inches (in reality, no 37-inch diameter is actually 37 inches tall), and 85 percent of 10 inches is 8.5 inches. Deflate the tire to the 85 percent height. Take note of the pressure, as this is your optimum pressure for normal rock-crawling and off-road situations.

If you are overlanding and add weight to your Jeep for a trip, make sure to adjust the tire pressure to compensate for the additional load. To put the difference between tire brands in perspective, we have seen as much as a 6-psi variance from a soft-sidewall tire to a very-stiff sidewall tire on the same corner of the same vehicle. One tire may be at optimum pressure at 15 psi, which means that beadlock rims are not necessary, while another tire on the same rig may need only 8 psi for the optimum pressure. Any pressure below 10 or 11 psi really should be using beadlock wheels for safety.

Another factor to consider is a new tire versus an older one that has been used for several hundred miles. Once a tire is broken in, recheck the sidewall measurements. The tire will become more flexible after driving off-road at low tire pressures.

Void Ratio and Tread Blocks

The void ratio of a tire describes how much of the surface of the tire tread is covered with tread blocks versus the area void of rubber. Higher void ratios mean less traction on hard surfaces but usually more traction on soft surfaces. Tread-block design affects traction and road noise. Taller tread blocks work better in soft surfaces, such as sand and mud, and especially soft silt.

The void ratio of a tire's tread measures the area of tread blocks versus the area of the gaps between the tread blocks (white in the illustration). All-terrain tires use a small void ratio, which means that more rubber is on the ground. Mud-terrain tires use much larger void ratios, which means that less rubber is on the ground but there is more ability for the tire to grip a surface, especially soft surfaces, such as mud, sand, and snow. Larger void ratios also create more noise on the highway.

Tire Diameter and Ground Clearance

A major reason to upgrade to larger tires is to gain ground clearance. However, for the reasons stated earlier, the ability to run at lower tire pressures is just as important. Closely related to tire diameter is the diameter of the wheel. The smaller the wheel, the larger the tire sidewall.

The smallest wheel that is practical on a Wrangler JL or Gladiator JT is 17 inches in diameter. A large-diameter wheel reduces sidewall height and the capacity to lower tire pressures. A 17-inch-diameter wheel is highly desirable for any size of tire, even a 40-inch-diameter monster, and tire pressures can be optimized for more traction and improved ride quality.

Tire Compliance Over Rocks and Obstacles

Often overlooked as an important tire characteristic is the ability of a tire to wrap around rocks and other obstacles. Airing down to optimum tire pressures allows this. Tire compliance is important when climbing up large rocks.

Undercut ledges can be very difficult to climb if the ledge is taller than the centerline of the wheel, say 24 inches tall with a 37-inch tire. The lip of the ledge is above the center of the tire, which means the tire must move backward to climb forward. The only way that this can happen is if the tire has a low enough tire pressure to conform to the rock.

As the tire wraps around the rock, the tire compresses and allows the Jeep to climb up the rock face. If the tire pressure is too high, the tire will not compress enough, and the tire will try to push the whole Jeep backward, which makes forward progress very difficult, if not impossible.

If the tire sidewall loses grip in this situation, the wheel could easily be damaged. (Photo Courtesy Toby Jho)

Sidewall compliance allows the sidewall of the tire to grip the face of the rock wall. Also note the siping on the tire tread. The small lateral sipes help forward grip, while the longitudinal sipes increase side grip. This helps keep the tire from sliding off tilted rock faces. (Photo Courtesy Toby Jho)

The ability of a tire to wrap around an undercut rock is critical, especially if the top of the undercut is taller than the mid-point of the tire. Tire pressure plays a key role.

Undercut rocks can be very difficult to climb. Tire flex is important. Lower tire pressures allow more tire sidewall flex.

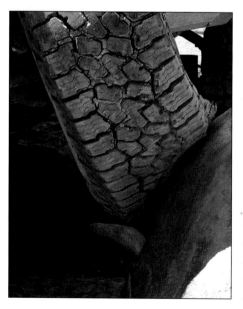

Tire grip on the side of a sloped rock can be the difference between clearing an obstacle and sliding off the rock. Sliding off the rock can cause the vehicle to become stuck and cause possible damage to rocker panels or other exposed body sections.

The Falken WildPeak MT tire has a fairly stiff sidewall, which requires lower aired-down tire pressures to achieve good sidewall flex compared to other similar tires with softer, more flexible sidewalls. At 10 psi and lower, bead-lock wheels are a necessity to ensure that the tire bead stays seated on the wheel rim.

All-Terrain versus Mud-Terrain Tires

The debate over mud-terrain versus all-terrain tires will never cease. Now, the debate is more clouded with the advent of the all-terrain hybrid tire. The hybrid tires fill the gap between a mud-terrain and an all-terrain tire.

A hybrid off-road tire will feature more aggressive tread blocks and a larger void ratio when compared to an all-terrain tire. The rubber compound is usually a little softer, so traction is better than a pure AT tire, but wear is worse. While there has never been a clear winner in this argument, there are many factors to take into account: highway versus off-road miles, weather conditions, terrain, road surface, noise, etc.

Two hybrid all-terrain tires, the Falken WildPeak AT 3W and the Mickey Thompson Baja ATZ P3, have blurred the line distinguishing all-terrain tires from mud-terrain tires even more. These new-generation AT tires offer aggressive tread patterns and sidewalls while retaining a

Mud-terrain tires, such as the Falken WildPeak M/T tire (left), are generally preferred for serious off-road JLs and JTs. They are especially good on soft surfaces where the large tread blocks and softer rubber compound can increase grip. They also look more aggressive. All-terrain tires, such as the BFG All-Terrain TA tire (middle), appeal to more casual use due to better wear and a quieter ride on the highway. While the AT tire may have a harder rubber compound, the increased tread area due to a smaller void ratio allows most AT tires to perform with the equivalent MT tire in most off-road conditions. The Mickey Thompson Baja ATZ03 (right) all-terrain tire blurs the line between mud- and all-terrain tires. More of a hybrid, the ATZ03 features large tread blocks, a smaller void ratio, numerous sipes in the tread blocks, and a rubber compound that is softer than a typical AT tire but harder than an MT. Many tires companies have introduced this style of hybrid all-terrain tire. This new category is often called extreme all-terrain.

The BFG All-Terrain TA KO2 tire (top left) has one of the more aggressive sidewall designs. The siping allows flex for better grip. The ridges between the sidewall tread blocks are stepped to help eject rocks and debris from the sidewall. The Mickey Thompson Baja ATZ P3 all-terrain tire (top right) has a sidewall design more like a mud-terrain tire. This sidewall design grips very well on rock edges and the sides of ruts where little or no tread is gripping the surface. The Falken WildPeak AT03 (bottom left) has a very aggressive sidewall for an all-terrain tire. The stepped ridges on the upper part of the sidewall grip the edges of rocks and slopes progressively better. They also dig into soft surfaces for even more bite. This AT tire (bottom right), the Nexen Roadian AT, has a conservative sidewall design, but the triangular-shaped scallops on the lower portion of the sidewall provide a surprising amount of grip on loose dirt and large, sloped rocks.

The Nitto Trail Grappler mud-terrain tire offers outstanding off-road performance in all conditions while still providing a relatively quiet ride on the highway. With a 21/32-inch tread depth, the Trail Grappler works exceptionally well in soft surface conditions, such as sand and silt.

The tread blocks on the Nexen Roadian MTX help the tire climb rock faces. The flexible sidewall design allows this tire to flex considerably even at 15 psi, making beadlock wheels unnecessary.

The Milestar Patagonia M/T tire has become very popular due to excellent off-road performance and a very reasonable price for large M/T tires. (Photo Courtesy Henry Valesquez)

The Mickey Thompson Baja Boss mud-terrain tire offers excellent flex at low tire pressures. The sidewalls flex both laterally and longitudinally, which helps the Baja Boss pull the JL up steep rocks and ledges. (Photo Courtesy Toby Jho)

The Falken WildPeak AT3W hybrid all-terrain tire provides excellent off-road performance, great traction in all conditions, and a quite ride on the highway. The WildPeak AT3W is standard equipment on the Gladiator Rubicon and Mojave models.

smaller void ratio for reduced noise on the highway and harder rubber compounds for better tire wear when compared to a mud-terrain tire.

Ply Ratings, Tire Cutting, and Slashing

Cutting or puncturing a tire tread or slashing a sidewall is fairly common off-road. Areas with sharp rocks are the most likely to cause problems. Two factors help reduce the possibility of serious tire damage: run only load range D or E tires and air down as described here.

Load range refers to the ply rating. Old bias-ply tires had a ply rating, up to 10 ply for light truck and off-road tires. With modern materials, fewer plys are needed to achieve the same strength and puncture resistance. A D rating is the equivalent of an 8-ply bias tire. An E rating is the equivalent of a 10-ply bias tire. Tires with these ratings provide the best protection off-road.

The BFG All-Terrain T/A tire is standard equipment on the Wrangler JL Rubicon models, including the new 392 Hemi engine option. (Photo Courtesy FCA US LLC)

The Falken WildPeak M/T tire is available on the Gladiator Rubicon models.

Reasons to Air Down Tires

Increasing the tire contact patch or footprint, increases traction, which is a great reason to air down tires. An additional reason is to improve ride comfort on rough terrain. It is impossible to use soft enough springs to make the ride comfortable. Since a tire sidewall is a spring, lower tire pressures improve ride comfort.

A third reason is to reduce the chance of a tire puncture. When a tire is at lower pressures, it is more compliant and better resists a puncture from rocks and sharp objects. Finally,

lower tire pressures reduce damage to the road surface. Studies have determined that running at lower pressures spreads the load on the tire over a greater area (larger tire contact patch), and this actually reduces damage to the road surface. Less damage translates into less erosion.

As a side note, we have observed (but not tested) that different tires on the same vehicle on the same stretch of road generate different amounts of dust. Various tire pressures on the same tire have the same effect. Lower pressures make less dust. The only downside to airing down is reduced ground clearance. A trick that we use if we get high centered on an obstacle and do not have enough traction to move forward or backward is to air up one or more tires to gain a little ground clearance.

Tire Deflator Types

Tire deflators are the easiest way to air down tires when hitting the trails. In general, there are three types of deflators. Many tire-pressure gauges have a release valve for letting air out of a tire. These are very slow and require constant attention.

Second are deflators that screw onto the valve stem and depress the spring-loaded valve core. These are adjustable for a minimum pressure when they shut off. They usually come in sets of two or four. They're

Tire deflators are a must for airing down tires to an optimum tire pressure for off-road. The RockJock Analog deflator is very fast and accurate. This style of deflator screws onto the valve stem. The plunger engages the valve core inside the valve stem. The core is then unscrewed and the knurled knob release valve is opened to allow air pressure to decrease rapidly. Once the desired air pressure is reached, the valve is closed, the valve core is screwed back into the stem, and the deflator is removed. When testing this deflator versus four of the screw-on deflators, one single RockJock deflator was faster, although it was much more hands on.

Many screw-on tire deflators are on the market. The Coyote deflators provide the most consistent air-down pressures and are very reliable. Many screw-on deflators require readjustment after a few uses. The Coyote deflators come with a lifetime warranty.

not much faster than a pressure gauge, but with four and automatic shut off, you can screw them on and walk away.

The third deflator screws onto the valve stem but unscrews the valve core from the stem while capturing it within the nozzle. It has a pressure gauge and on-off pressure-relief valve for accurate control of tire pressure. This allows for very rapid airing down. One of these deflators is typically faster than four of the others. The downside is the need to watch the pressure as it drops.

Viair makes portable 12-volt compressors as well as complete on-board air compressor systems. The top-end system features a dual compressor and an air tank for quicker airing up.

The central valve on the Speedflate system allows all four tires to be deflated at once. Plug in an air source, either a compressor or a Power Tank, at the valve fitting to air up tires. The pressure equalizes on all four tires. (Photo Courtesy Speedflate)

Power Tank offers a nice, clean mounting bracket for the 10-pound version of the Power Tank in Wrangler JL models. The mount uses existing holes in the Wrangler roll cage, which makes installation a breeze. Mounts are available for both driver- and passenger-side mounting locations.

The Speedflate air system offers a very convenient way to air down and air up tires. The system uses a series of hoses connecting all four tire valves to a central valve. All four tires are deflated or inflated at once. (Photo Courtesy Speedflate)

The Apex Performance Rapid Precision Valve allows for speedy tire deflation and inflation. The Rapid Precision Valve replaces the standard valve stem and core. (Photo Courtesy Apex Performance)

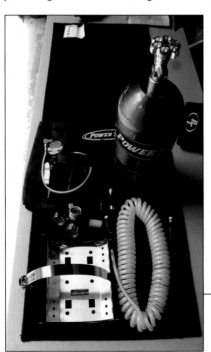

Power Tank offers a wide range of carbon dioxide tanks, regulators, mounts, hoses, gauges, and accessories. The Power Tank is the fastest way to air up tires. It uses compressed carbon dioxide to air up tires or drive air tools. We aired up all four 37-inch tires from 14 to 30 psi in about 3 minutes, which included moving from tire to tire. This compares to about 20 minutes with an on-board air compressor. The Power Tank is also quieter and more reliable than an electric air compressor. The downside is the need to refill the tank with carbon dioxide, which is available from paintball shops, some welding-supply shops, and beverage-dispensing equipment stores.

Another style of system uses four hoses and a manifold to air down all four tires at once. This system works with compressors or with a Power Tank. This adds to the ease and speed of altering tire pressures and has the added advantage of equalizing the pressure in all four tires. One such system is called Speedflate.

By using a tire-pressure gauge on the Apex Performance Rapid Precision Valve and opening the gate, the tire pressure is reduced rapidly. We aired down a 37-inch tire from 32 to 14 psi in less than 15 seconds.

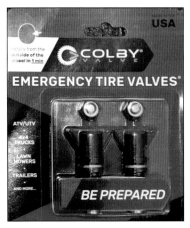

Colby Valve offers Emergency Tire Valves to replace broken valve stems without removing the tire and wheel from the vehicle and dismounting the tire. This clever product can come in handy on the trail. Many wheels offer little protection for the valve stem, which can be easily lopped off in rocky trail conditions.

Airing Up Tires

Reinflating tires before hitting the asphalt reduces the risk of a tire failure. A low tire will easily overheat if the distance and the speeds are too high. Driving short distances at lower speeds on days where the temperature is moderate is acceptable, but airing tires back up to normal highway pressure is very important.

There are two ways to air up tires. The first is by using a compressor. On-board compressors are the best option. Portable compressors are less expensive but overheat easily. Pay attention to the duty cycle. Do not run compressors too long, as damage can result. On-board compressors are convenient but operate slowly and are noisy.

Another option is a carbon dioxide tank, such as the Power Tank, which is the fastest way to air up tires. Power Tank offers a monster valve that allows for even faster airing up (and down as well). The downside to a Power Tank is the need to be refilled with carbon dioxide. The speed and convenience of airing up at the end of a day on the trail has made the Power Tank a popular airing-up option.

Wheels

Wheel selections for the Wrangler JL and Gladiator JT are in the hundreds—if not the thousands. When upgrading wheels, several choices must be made: aluminum alloy versus steel, wheel diameter and width, backspacing, and the standard versus beadlock design. Other factors when selecting wheels include tire size, tire clearance, and valve stem vulnerability. Lug hole configurations come into play only if axles are changed.

Aluminum alloy wheels are by far the most common wheels used on Wrangler JLs and Gladiator JTs. The Jesse Spade wheel from Rugged Ridge offers a variety of finish colors. We have tested this non-beadlock wheel to a low pressure of 10 psi on extreme rock-crawling terrain with no unseating of the tire bead from the rim.

Alloy Versus Steel

The two materials used in the manufacturing of wheels offer different advantages. Steel is less expensive. It is also strong and malleable, meaning that the wheel will bend on impact (not crack or break). A bent steel wheel can be hammered back (although with great difficulty) into a reasonable shape to hold air if deformed on the trail. A cracked or broken alloy wheel cannot be repaired. Any wheel can be (and probably will be) scratched, gouged, or more severely damaged when off-roading, especially on the extreme rock-crawling trails.

Alloy wheels are lighter for the same size and strength. Alloy wheels offer an extensive range of styles. Aluminum alloy wheels also dissipate heat better than steel, which helps to cool brakes under extreme conditions. The cost varies considerably with alloy wheels.

Measuring Tire Heights

To optimize aired-down tire pressures, knowing the tire dimensions is critical. The formula for airing down requires a measurement of the tire sidewall from the bottom of the rim (or beadlock ring) to the ground at full inflation. The pressure is reduced to 85 percent of that measurement for general off-road driving and most rock-crawling situations. For soft surfaces, such as mud, deep snow, and especially sand, the tire pressure can be reduced to about 75 percent of the full-inflation sidewall height.

In the tire specification sheet for a given tire, the diameter is one of the measurements. This is the height of the tire inflated to the maximum-rated tire pressure with no load on the tire. The sidewall (from the bottom of the rim to the ground) decreases when the tire is installed on the vehicle under full static load.

In our example, we use the Mickey Thompson Baja Boss mud-terrain tire. The tires were broken in so that the height measurements are more accurate.

Tire Specifications Example	
Brand	Mickey Thompson
Model	Baja Boss M/T
Size	40x13.50R17LT
Tire diameter (static)	Listed as 39.8 inches (actual measurement was 39.75 inches). On a Jeep Wrangler JL Sport S Unlimited left front corner, the loaded tire diameter was 39.35 inches (just under 1/2-inch sidewall compression) at 35 psi (maximum rated pressure).
Beadlock ring	17.75 inches tall
Bottom of beadlock ring to ground (at 35 psi)	10.56 inches (10.56 x 0.85 = 8.96 inches, rounded to 9 inches)
Pressure needed to reach 9-inch sidewall height	7 psi

The 7-psi aired-down pressure indicates a stiff sidewall tire and the need to use beadlock wheels.

This compares to the Nexen Roadian MTX 37 x 12.50 R17 tire on the same corner of the same Jeep, which required only 14 psi to air down to the 85-percent mark. At that pressure, beadlocks are unnecessary. ■

The Mickey Thompson Baja Boss M/T 40 x 13.50R17LT requires a tire pressure of 7 psi to achieve a good sidewall bulge for normal off-road driving. This low pressure requires a beadlock wheel for retaining the tire on the wheel.

The Mickey Thompson Baja Boss M/T 40 x 13.50R17LT has good sidewall flex at low tire pressures. To achieve the 85-percent sidewall measurement on this tire, it requires a tire pressure of 7 psi.

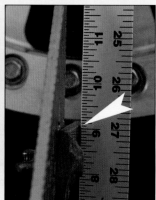

The sidewall height on the Mickey Thompson Baja Boss M/T 40 x 13.50R17LT at maximum pressure under load is 10-5/8 inches from the bottom of the beadlock ring to the ground.

The 85-percent measurement for this tire is 9 inches. The tire pressure to reach this height is 7 psi.

Mickey Thompson Baja Boss Tire Review

Mickey Thompson tires provide excellent off-road performance and durability. The Mickey Thompson Baja Boss is the third off-road tire that we tested from the company. Each type of tire from Mickey Thompson has performed extremely well off-road with good highway manners. The ATZ p3 hybrid tire is one of the best compromises. It offers outstanding off-road performance and a relatively quiet highway noise level and good handling on the pavement.

The latest offering from Mickey Thompson is the Baja Boss mud-terrain tire. The 40x13.50R17LT Baja Boss is ideal for the Wrangler JL build with the Yukon-equipped Currie 60 Extreme axles and the PSC power steering. The

The sidewall lugs on the Baja Boss tires provide plenty of grip to hold laterally on rock faces. (Photo Courtesy Toby Jho)

hardware is capable of handling the impressive traction and loads created by the Baja Boss tires.

Most of the four-wheeling activities with the project JL involve rock crawling with some higher-speed desert running and also highway driving. The big 40-inch tires work well in the rocks, almost making big rocks too easy to tackle. Forward bite is excellent, and the lateral traction ensures that sliding sideways off big rocks is not likely. The tires are heavy, which requires a low air-down tire pressure. In the case of our JL, we needed to air down to 7 psi to get a good tire contact patch spread. The low pressure really requires good beadlocks, such as the Raceline Monster beadlocks. ■

Steep descents and climbs on steep rock faces such as Chicken Rock at Cougar Buttes require excellent forward traction. The Mickey Thompson Baja Boss 40s use a tread block design with siping to improve traction. The Baja Boss tires make this climb and descent almost too easy. (Photo Courtesy Toby Jho)

Specifications	
Brand	Mickey Thompson
Model	Baja Boss
Size	40x13.50R17LT
Load range	C
Max load	3,195 pounds at 35 psi
Height	39.8 inches
Section width	13.6 inches
Width	11.0 inches
Weight	95 pounds

The Baja Boss features a very aggressive sidewall with thick, tall lugs for great sidewall traction. Next-generation four-pitch Sidebiters are 50-percent larger than any previous Mickey Thompson radial tire, providing significant off-road traction improvements.

A great rock-crawling tire must be able to conform to the rocks when climbing to maximize traction. The distortion of the sidewall on the Mickey Thompson Baja Boss tire not only conforms to the rock profile but also helps pull the Jeep up the rock.

The asymmetrical tread pattern on the Baja Boss helps reduce noise and improves traction and on-center steering feel. Mickey Thompson's PowerPly XD uses thicker denier cord to provide greater puncture resistance, improved handling, and quicker steering response than the original PowerPly technology.

Nexen Roadian MTX Tire Review

After initial preproduction product testing and more than three years of running on the Nexen Roadian MTX mud-terrain tires, their performance, durability, and wear stand out.

The Nexen Roadian MTX tires have been tested in just about every conceivable situation both on and off-road. They are excellent on the rocks, really good in sand and mud, and absorb rough terrain when aired down. On the highway, handling is excellent, and noise, while not the quietest mud-terrain tire ever, is relatively quiet. Wear on the Nexen Roadian MTX is excellent. We have used them on five Jeeps, plus five rental Jeeps.

The rental Jeeps were going through a set of tires every six months prior to switching to the Nexens. Now, the Jeeps can go for 1 to 1½ years before needing new tires. The rental company has had zero tire failures in the two-plus years it used the Nexen Roadian MTX. The sidewall design on the Nexen Roadian MTX allows a good tire footprint when aired down to 14 psi on our JL project. The sidewalls are flexible, even though the tire is F rated. Beadlock wheels are not needed for these tires on a heavy Jeep. ∎

Traction in loose dirt and deep ruts requires a tire with good compliance and aggressive tread blocks.

Climbing undercut rocks needs great flex in the tire sidewall. The Nexen Roadian MTX on this rock flexes easily at 14 psi to maneuver up the rock face.

Specifications	
Brand	Nexen
Model	Roadian MTX
Size	37 x 12.50R17LT
Load Range	F
Max load	3,195 pounds at 80 psi
Height	36.8 inches
Section width	12.5 inches
Width	10.0 inches

The Nexen Roadian MTX tread block design is symmetrical. The overlapping tread blocks help reduce noise. The longitudinal siping on the tread blocks improves forward grip, while the lateral siping adds greatly to side grip. (Photo Courtesy Toby Jho)

The sidewall cord construction allows the Nexen Roadian MTX to flex over rocks at a higher tire pressure than many other mud-terrain tires. Tire conformity helps control speed when descending steep ledges.

The Nexen Roadian MTX features a unique sidewall design on either side of the tire, allowing some customization. Even though the sidewall designs are different, the sidewall grip is outstanding on side slopes and vertical rock ledges.

The Raceline-simulated beadlock alloy wheel is offered in a selection of finishes, diameters, and bolt patterns. With the Nexen Roadian MTX mud-terrain tire, a non-beadlock wheel works well because the sidewalls flex. This wheel-and-tire combination is normally run at 14 psi for most trail conditions.

The Raceline Hostage simulated beadlock wheels have seen some extreme trail duty on Quinn's Gladiator project.

Jeep offers a selection of alloy wheels on various models of Wranglers and Gladiators. The Willys version of the Gladiator features a Mopar alloy wheel wrapped in a BFG KM2 mud-terrain tire. (Photo Courtesy FCA US LLC)

The 2021 Wrangler Rubicon features an alloy wheel with the BFG KO2 All-Terrain tire. Jeep and Mopar have stepped up their game on the 2021-and-newer Wranglers and Gladiators. (Photo Courtesy FCA US LLC)

Alloy wheel manufacturing uses four different processes: forging, high-pressure die casting, low-pressure die casting, and gravity casting. Forged wheels are the toughest and strongest, but they are also much more expensive. Many forged wheels are not street legal and are mostly used for competition.

Cast wheels are by far the most common. The casting process is less important than the quality of the materials used in the process. Although it is rare, cast wheels can crack or even break from hard impacts off-road.

Standard Bead Versus Beadlocks

Close manufacturing tolerances for current wheels and tires allow a very tight fit between the wheel bead and the tire bead. For this reason, most Wrangler JL and Gladiator JT owners can use a standard-bead wheel (like the stock wheels).

Beadlock-style wheels look like beadlocks but have a standard wheel bead. A true beadlock wheel has an outer ring that bolts to the wheel. The beadlock rings hold the tire bead in place so that it cannot become dislodged from the wheel at low pressures in extreme conditions.

We have tested many tires on standard rims down to 10 psi for soft surface, low-speed four-wheeling. This is usually a low enough pressure for adequate traction. A rule of thumb for tire pressures on a standard, non-beadlock rim is a minimum of 10

The stock alloy wheels on the Jeep Gladiator Mojave edition provide protection for the valve stem in the rocks and also look great. (Photo Courtesy FCA US LLC)

The Falken WildPeak AT3W all-terrain tires are mounted to the 2021 Gladiator Mojave alloy wheels. This hybrid AT tire is one of our favorites. (Photo Courtesy FCA US LLC)

KMC Wheels offers the XD228 Machete beadlock wheel made from cast aluminum, which is ideal for extreme rock crawling. An 8-on-6.5-inch bolt pattern is used on several axle upgrades, such as the Currie 60 Extreme axle assemblies.

RBP is fairly new to the beadlock market, although it has been manufacturing large wheels for the truck market for many years. The new RBP 50R Cobra Dual-Purpose Beadlock Wheel can be used as a traditional non-beadlock or as a true beadlock wheel. (Photo Courtesy Henry Valesquez)

Mopar offers some nice-looking optional wheels for the Wrangler JL and Gladiator JT. (Photo Courtesy FCA US LLC)

Raceline makes beadlock wheels for many applications in off-road racing. The Raceline Monster beadlock with Mickey Thompson 40 x 13.50-17 Baja Boss mud-terrain tires creates considerable traction. The strength of the eight-lug wheels on big axles reduces the chance of axle stud or wheel failure.

RBP Wheels, along with several other beadlock wheel makers, offer beadlock rings in both steel and aluminum. The aluminum rings can be anodized or powder coated in a wide range of colors for a customized look.

Beadlock wheels sold through Jeep dealers was unheard of before 2021. Mopar now makes a true beadlock wheel for the Wrangler JL and Gladiator JT. (Photo Courtesy FCA US LLC)

KMC Wheels is another manufacturer offering a great line of beadlock wheels for a variety of off-road and racing applications. The Nitto Trail Grappler tires have an impeccable reputation for off-road performance.

This steel beadlock wheel looks like a homemade modification for a standard steel wheel. The beadlock ring uses only 16 bolts to hold it in place. Most beadlocks use 32 bolts to secure the beadlock ring in place. It is important to use quality materials that are properly engineered. A home-built beadlock is not a sound idea. And it is important to check the torque every 30 days to verify that the beadlock ring is secure.

Torque all of the bolts on the beadlock ring. It is best to torque in two or three steps. With the Raceline beadlocks, the first torque step is about 14 ft-lbs. The final torque is 17 ft-lbs. After a few miles of driving, recheck the torque. The beadlock bolts should be retorqued every 30 to 60 days.

psi. Extreme situations, such as deep snow, or wet, muddy, or snow-covered rocks, require lower pressures, as do tires with a very stiff sidewall. Here is where beadlocks are necessary.

We tested beadlocks at tire pressures as low as 3 psi in snow; on sand and mud; and on snowy, muddy rocks on black-diamond trails. Beadlocks require proper installation and maintenance. Most beadlocks have 32 bolts holding the outer ring in place. The bolts must be installed in the proper sequence and to the correct torque.

We torque in three stages: 12 ft-lbs, progressing to 14 ft-lbs, and ending at 16 ft-lbs. We then double-check the torque of all bolts. Various wheel manufacturers may have different torque specifications. Check the torque settings monthly to ensure reliability and safety. All bolts should be replaced annually.

Wheel Diameter

Stock wheels on the Wrangler JL and Gladiator JT have a 17-inch diameter, except the Sahara models, which are equipped with 18-inch wheels. The smallest-diameter wheel that will fit on a Wrangler JL or Gladiator JT is 17 inches due to brake-rotor and caliper-clearance issues. The ideal wheel diameter is 17 inches, the smallest possible wheel diameter that fits. A larger-diameter wheel means a shorter sidewall dimension for a given tire.

Since 37-inch-diameter tires are common on the Wrangler JL and Gladiator JT, we will use that diameter as an example. Referring back to the tire-pressure section earlier, reducing tire pressures off-road is a function of the tire sidewall height and other factors, including weight on the tire and tire sidewall stiffness. We generally use an 85-percent measurement for sidewall reduction for most off-road driving situations.

A 37-inch-diameter tire on a 17-inch-diameter wheel has about a 10-inch sidewall height. Regardless of the tire brand or model, the ideal sidewall height is about 8.5 inches. If a 20-inch-diameter wheel is used, the sidewall height is now only 8.5 inches at full pressure. Reducing the sidewall height to the ideal 85-percent number is about a 7.25-inch sidewall height. This number requires a much higher tire pressure to ensure that the tire is not damaged by being pinched between the wheel rim and the ground or a rock. The higher tire pressure reduces the tire footprint and traction, increases ride harshness, and increases the risk of tire damage.

Wheel Width

Stock wheel widths are 7.5 inches. The stock wheel width works fine on tires up to about 8.5 inches wide, which includes 32- to 33-inch-diameter tires. Larger tires, such as a 12.50 section width, should use a wheel width of 8.5 to 10 inches.

Bolt Pattern

The Wrangler JL and Gladiator JT use the same wheel bolt pattern as the Wrangler JK, which is a 5-on-5 bolt pattern. This means that there are 5 lug holes in a 5-inch bolt circle.

Offset and Backspacing

Wheel backspacing is critical on the Wrangler JL and Gladiator JT. Backspacing is measured from the back of the wheel rim to the surface where the wheel mounts to the hub. Too much backspacing with larger,

Wheel backspacing is critical. It is measured from the back of the wheel rim to where the wheel mounts to the hub. Too much backspacing with larger, wider tires can cause rubbing problems while the front tires are turned near full lock and at the extremes of vertical suspension travel.

The optimal backspacing for 8.5- to 9.0-inch-wide wheels is 3.5 to 4.75 inches. The smaller the backspacing measurement, the more the tire will stick out from the vehicle. The Raceline Monster beadlock has 4.5 inches of backspacing.

The lug nut key socket is used with anti-theft lug nuts. Carry the lug nut key socket in your Jeep if you use security lug nuts.

wider tires can cause rubbing problems when the front tires are turned near full lock and at the extremes of vertical suspension travel. Optimum backspacing for 8.5- to 9.0-inch-wide wheels is 3.5 to 4.75 inches.

The smaller the backspacing measurement, the more the tire will stick out away from the vehicle. This puts additional load on the wheel hubs and bearings.

On a 9-inch-wide wheel with 4.5-inch backspacing, the center of the wheel interface with the hub is in the center of the wheel, and the load on the wheel bearings is not increased. Wider tires require less backspacing. A solution to avoid this

requires an axle swap. For example, the Currie 60 Extreme axles are 70 inches wide compared to the stock 66.5-inch width on a JL. The JK front axle width is 65.5 inches.

Wheel Weight

Wheel weight is important, but given that off-road tires are heavy and the Jeep Wrangler JL and Gladiator JT use solid axles, the effect of wheel weight is minimal compared to the total unsprung weight of the wheels, tires, axle housings, gears, and half the weight of suspension components.

The most common wheel size for a JL with larger AT or MT tires is 17-inches in diameter with an 8.5- to 9.0-inch width. A typical steel wheel weighs around 40 pounds; an alloy wheel in the mid to high 20-pound range and an alloy beadlock with a steel retaining ring weighs about 44 pounds.

Wheel and Tire Balancing

Out-of-balance tires lead to damaged tires and a rough ride. In addition, death wobble can be caused by out-of-balance tires. On the Wrangler JL and Gladiator JT, especially with larger tires, static balancing is not adequate. The Jeep factory uses dynamic balancing. Dynamic bal-

This 37-inch BFG MT tire and Raceline beadlock wheel measured less than 2 ounces out of balance on the first spin after mounting. After adding weights, the second spin showed nearly perfect balance at 0.25 ounces out on the inner rim. Perfect balance was achieved on the third spin. The fallacy that beadlock wheels are impossible to balance is inaccurate

Jeep uses dynamic wheel balancing for the Wrangler JL and Gladiator JT. The reason is simple: with large tires and high rotational inertia due to the heavy tire tread located away from the center of rotation, dynamic balancing reduces out-of-balance issues, such as shimmy and death wobble. The tire and wheel are spun at high speed until the location of imbalance is located on both the inside and outside of the rim.

ancing balances both the outside and the inside of the rim, which reduces wheel wobble and shimmy.

Wheel Spacers and Adapters

Wheel spacers that slip over the wheel studs can cause issues. Wheel adapters that have built-in wheel studs and bolt onto the wheel studs on the hub work better and are safer. Check the regulations in your state because they are not legal in some states.

BUMPERS, ARMOR, AND PROTECTION

Off-road driving presents many hazards with the potential to damage a Wrangler JL or Gladiator JT. For this reason, these Jeep models come equipped with some underside skidplate protection. Sheet-metal skidplates protect the fuel tank and transfer case on all models.

Critical components, such as the engine and transmission oil pans, are left unprotected. The muffler at the rear of the Wrangler models is also exposed to trail damage. The FAD as well as the front sway-bar disconnect system can be damaged on Rubicon models. The diesel and hybrid versions are equipped with additional at-risk components. Rubicon models are equipped with rock sliders to protect the rocker panels from very expensive damage. Other models leave the rocker panels exposed.

The stock plastic bumper covers offer very little protection and are susceptible to damage. The optional steel bumpers are adequate for protection but not ideal for the extreme off-roading situations. Stock fenders are easily damaged. Inner fender liners are prone to tire-rub damage when larger tires are fitted. Control-arm and shock-absorber mounts are exposed to damage, especially on the axle

The Jeep Wrangler JL and Gladiator JT aftermarket offers a wide range of fenders, underside protection, and armor. Larger tires and extreme terrain require upgrades to avoid damage and improve performance. (Photo Courtesy Toby Jho)

housings. Fortunately, the Jeep aftermarket offers a wide range of products to provide additional protection with styling to suit almost any taste.

Skidplates

While the stock skidplates provide some protection, they also have protrusions that can catch on rocks and large bumps. The ultimate solution for protection and a smooth skidplate surface that will slide across rocks and obstacles is a full belly-pan skidplate system. Companies such as Rock Hard 4x4 and Artec Industries offer complete belly-pan systems in aluminum and steel for both the Wrangler JL and Gladiator JT.

A wide range of individual skidplates is offered to protect the gas tank, transfer case, evaporative canister, muffler, front sway-bar disconnect, FAD, front air dam, and front

The underside protection on the stock Wrangler JL and Gladiator JT leaves a lot to be desired in rocky terrain. The stock front crossmember on the Gladiator has been damaged from rock crawling.

Rock Hard 4x4 makes a complete belly-pan skidplate system for both the Wrangler JL and Gladiator JT. The belly pan protects all of the critical components under the Jeeps. The systems are available in both steel and aluminum plate.

The Artec Industries full-aluminum belly pan uses a much stronger crossmember. The transfer-case skidplate bolts to the crossmember. Additional skidplates integrate into the system for a smooth underside installation.

and rear lower control arm brackets. More than two dozen companies offer a variety of skidplates for underside protection.

The stock sheet metal skidplates provide some protection for the fuel tank and the transfer case, but the engine and transmission oil pans are susceptible to damage even during moderate off-roading. While other components can be damaged, engine and transmission oil-pan damage can cause a breakdown and expensive repairs. For any type of off-road use, adding an engine and transmission skidplate is a high priority. The low-hanging muffler on the Wrangler JL is likely to sustain damage.

Skidplates are available from several resources, but replacing the muffler with a catback exhaust system is an alternative because the muffler is replaced and relocated. The lower control-arm brackets are also very vulnerable in rock-crawling situations. Skidplates for the control arms are offered by several companies. Rock Hard 4x4 makes a bolt-on set for both front and rear control-arm mounts.

The Artec Industries full-aluminum belly-pan system covers all critical components under the Gladiator. The access hole allows easy oil changes. The aluminum belly pan adds only 20 pounds to the weight of the Gladiator after the stock skidplates are removed.

Control arm mounts are vulnerable to damage in rough and rocky terrain. Several companies offer control arm and shock mount skidplates.

The muffler on the Wrangler JL is not protected. The Gladiator muffler is mounted within the frame. Rough Country and several other companies offer muffler skidplates.

Rock Sliders

The rocker panels are easily damaged. Repairs are difficult and expensive. Rock sliders, also called rocker slides, protect the vulnerable rocker panels below the doors on all Wrangler JL and Gladiator JT models. Some current models are equipped with rock sliders that offer some protection.

For extreme off-road driving, robust sliders are a great idea. Rock sliders take a real beating in extreme situations. For this reason, they need to be made from very durable, heavy-duty materials. Sliders can be made from formed steel plate or heavy-wall steel tubing. In addition, sliders should bolt to the frame rails. Some sliders have additional mounting points on the body to help stabilize the slider, but these can cause body damage.

The stock rock sliders found on some Wrangler JL and Gladiator JT models fit nearly flush with the body. While they offer protection from vertical impacts, they offer no protection to the side. For example, sliding off of a rock sideways can cause the vehicle to tilt into a rock or tree. Rock sliders that protrude away from the body offer additional protection in these situations.

Rock sliders are available from a wide range of companies. The Rock Slide Engineering step sliders offer a unique take on rock sliders that feature built-in retractable steps. While several companies offer retractable steps for the Wrangler JL and Gladiator JT, they are not sturdy rock sliders and can be easily damaged in extreme terrain. The Rock Slide Engineering

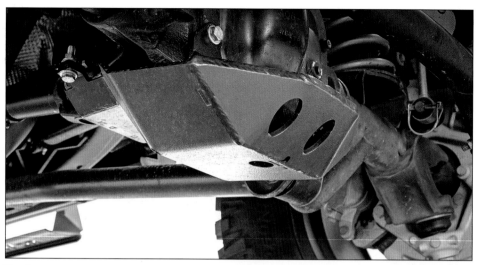

The lowest points on any Wrangler JL or Gladiator JT (except tires) are the front and rear differential housings. Currie 60 Extreme axles come with differential housing skidplates. In addition to protecting the differential housing, the skidplate allows the axle housing to slide more easily over rocks and large bumps. Several companies offer differential skids for most of the axles used on the Gladiator JT and Wrangler JL.

Rock sliders protect the vulnerable rocker panels. The Rugged Ridge XHD Rock Sliders protrude away from the body to offer additional protection from rock or tree damage when the Jeep tilts or slides off of rocks. The vertical plate does not bolt to the body, so nutserts and drilling are unnecessary. Felt padding on the slider protects the body paint from rubbing scars.

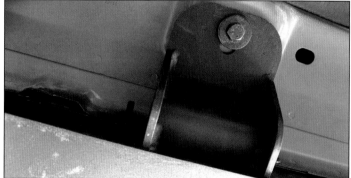

The Rugged Ridge rock sliders bolt to the frame in existing holes so no drilling is required.

Rock Slide Engineering Slider Steps bolt to the frame. Earlier versions for the Wrangler JK featured vertical plates along the rocker panels that required drilling and the use of nutserts for attachment. The Wrangler JL and Gladiator JT versions do not have the vertical plate, which reduces body damage when the slider flexes.

Rock Slide Engineering Slider Steps use a retractable step that deploys when the doors are opened and retracts when the doors are closed. The Rock Slide Engineering Slider Steps are strong rock sliders rated for moderate black-diamond trails.

Rock Slide Engineering Slider Steps have an optional skidplate system that is made of 3/16-inch steel plate. The skidplates protect the entire slider structure except for the retractable step opening. The skidplates are intended to provide extra protection on the most extreme rock-crawling trails.

Step Sliders are very strong and even offer an add-on skidplate for additional protection in the rocks.

Body Armor

Body armor protects the rear corners and quarter panels of the body. Armor is made from aluminum, steel, or plastic. Taillight guards are also available. While some of these products are heavy duty and can protect the body from dents, the primary job of this type of protection is to protect the paint and easily damaged components from rocks, heavy brush, and tree branches. Several companies offer a variety of body armor and protection.

Fenders

Wrangler JL and Gladiator JT Rubicon models feature highline fenders that offer more tire clear-ance than non-Rubicon models. This reduces the need for aftermarket fenders to fit larger tires. Aftermarket fenders offer additional tire clearance for larger tires and the option to personalize the style for individual tastes. Both front and rear fenders are available in wide and narrow designs.

The narrow designs do not cover the tires completely, which causes water, mud, and snow to spray. Many states require mud flaps if the tires are not fully covered by fenders. Most of the flat fender designs not only allow more tire clearance but also have the retro flat-fender look of the original World War II Jeeps. Plastic composite fenders are also available from MCE. Although, as of this writing, Wrangler JL and Gladiator JT fenders are in development. The MCE fenders are flexible and reduce the chance of damage on the trail.

Stock fenders can also be modified for more clearance and improved looks. When modifying a stock front fender, a turn signal and nighttime running light may need to be added. Kits such as the Rugged Ridge Front Fender Chop Brackets with running lights solve this problem.

The stock fender liners offer protection from rocks and road debris but are shaped in such a way that

When the stock inner fender liners are removed, many vulnerable components are exposed. The plastic stock liners do not offer sufficient clearance for larger tires (37-inch-plus diameters). Several companies offer sheet-metal inner-fender-liner kits that provide better clearance and protection.

Rugged Ridge HD Steel Tube front fenders improve tire clearance, especially on non-Rubicon models. The tubular edge adds rigidity and strength to the fender. The flat fender design adds a retro CJ look to a modern Jeep.

GenRight manufactures a stylish aluminum flat fender with a tubular ridge for both the Gladiator JT and Wrangler JL. The GenRight inner fender liner improves tire clearance and adds a finished appearance to the fender.

Rugged Ridge HD Steel Tube rear fenders match the front fenders. Improved tire clearance is an additional benefit. The narrow version of a rear fender may require the use of mud flaps in some states.

Rugged Ridge aluminum front inner fender liners protect vulnerable components inside the engine compartment. The inner fender liner design combined to the Rugged Ridge HD Steel Tube front fenders improve tire clearance considerably over stock fenders and inner liners.

GenRight aluminum rear fenders match the look of the front fenders. Inner liners add a finished look to the Gladiator. Similar fenders are available for the JL.

Rugged Ridge Front Fender Chop Brackets with daytime running lights allow trimming the stock front fenders on the Rubicon Jeep Wrangler JL for improved clearance. The small LED light functions as both a running light and a turn-signal light. It is surprisingly bright.

Bumpers can be made from fabricated steel and aluminum or formed under extreme pressure from either material. Full-width front bumpers provide tire protection in brush but limit rock-crawling capabilities. Stubby front bumpers allow for up to a 90-degree approach angle when climbing a single rock or when the Jeep is angled so that a large rock is approached one tire at a time.

Most aftermarket front bumpers come equipped with shackle mounts. Bull bars, strikers, and stingers add more protection for grilles and winches as well as good mounting points for lights. These add-ons are

they tend to rub with larger tires during full steering lock and full articulation. Electrical connections, wires, and tubes are exposed without inner fender protection. It was possible to eliminate inner fender liners on the JK, but many more components are exposed on the Wrangler JL and Gladiator JT. Aftermarket fender inner liners are available from companies such as Rugged Ridge, GenRight, Rough Country, and several others.

Bumpers

Jeep stepped up its game by offering steel bumpers on some Wrangler JL and Gladiator JT models. Mopar also offers aftermarket bumpers through Jeep dealers and other retailers. Steel or aluminum front bumpers facilitate winch mounting. Rear bumpers can be upgraded for more durability and to support the weight and size of larger spare tires.

Front Bumpers

Front bumpers come in full-width and narrow or stubby widths. Modular front bumpers allow a stubby bumper to become a full-width bumper or something in between by adding bolt-on sections to the narrow bumper. Most aftermarket front bumpers easily accommodate winches, lights, and D-rings or soft shackles for recovery.

One of the modular front bumpers is the MetalCloak frame-built bumper. The MetalCloak bumper features extended, bolt-on end caps with receptacles for the stock or aftermarket fog lights. The end caps can be removed to make the bumper a stubby, narrow front bumper for improved rock-crawling capability.

Bestop offers bumpers for the Wrangler JL and Gladiator JT, including the Highrock 4x4 front bumper. The Highrock bumper is available in a modular design, offering several options and looks. This bumper is equipped with the Baja Designs Squadron lights and a Warn Zeon 10S winch. (Photo Courtesy Bestop)

often options that can be bolted or welded to the bumper.

Winch Mounts

Most aftermarket front bumpers feature mounts for winches. Some winches need additional mounting plates. Be aware that not all winches have the same mounting bolt pattern, so check. In addition, some winches will not fit on some bumpers due to clearance issues with the grille.

Some front bumpers mount the winch low on the bumper, keeping weight lower and improving airflow to the radiator. Winches place extremely heavy loads on the bumper and the frame. Be sure that the mounting points are very strong for the winch and the bumper.

Rear Bumpers

Rear bumpers are available in many styles. Rear bumpers need to

The Rugged Ridge HD Stubby front bumper is made from formed steel. The bumper utilizes two shackle brackets with dual mounting holes. The winch mount is integrated into the bumper. An optional Rugged Ridge HD-X Striker Bar can be added.

Jeep Wrangler JL and Gladiator JT Rubicon models feature a Mopar steel front bumper with a removable extension for a stubby bumper alternative. The steel bumper makes winch installations easy. (Photo Courtesy FCA US LLC)

Rough Country offers a unique stubby front bumper called the Trail Bumper. The bumper comes with integrated flush-mount LED cube lights installed as well as a bull bar with a 20-inch LED light bar. A front bumper skidplate is included as well as shackle brackets and a winch mount.

The Rugged Ridge HD-X Striker Bar can be bolted to the Rugged Ridge HD Stubby front bumper or welded in place as shown here.

The Rugged Ridge HD rear bumper allows the installation of larger tires on the stock spare tire carrier. The bumper also features shackle mounts and cutouts for a Hi-Lift jack. Installation is a simple bolt-in operation.

Casey Currie manufactures the CRC rear bumper for the Wrangler JL. This bumper features a depression for larger tires that includes a drain to eliminate water buildup.

Tire carriers come in two styles. Some swing out with the tailgate; others swing out separately. Those that swing with the door are more convenient but also cost more. Due to the increased strength of the Wrangler JL rear door hinges compared to the JK hinges, tire carriers are available for mounting to the rear door, which eliminates the need for a bumper-mounted tire carrier. Bumper-mounted tire carriers work well as long as the tire carrier mount to the bumper is strong enough to handle the heavy load of a larger wheel and tire.

Other Mounts

Many rear bumpers have built-in and optional mounts for Hi-Lift jacks, Pull Pal ground anchors, fuel/water cans/tanks, shovel and axes, and antenna mounts for CB or Ham radios. These mounts can be very convenient for quick access and

be sturdy for rock crawling because they often make impact with large rocks when dropping off a rock or ledge or scrape when climbing. Most rear bumpers are designed to provide better departure angles than stock.

Stock bumpers are really unsuitable for extreme trail conditions. As with front bumpers, rear bumpers are made from steel and aluminum and can be fabricated or formed. Light mounts and D-ring and soft shackle mounts are included in some bumpers, but they are optional on others.

Tire Mounts

The Wrangler JL spare tire mounts to the rear door. Compared to the Wrangler JK, the JL mount is sturdier and can accommodate a slightly

larger tire. The Gladiator JT spare tire mounts under the bed. Spare-tire carriers that mount the spare in the bed are available. Some Wrangler JL rear bumpers include a tire carrier.

The Spartacus HD Tire Carrier Kit by Rugged Ridge allows a larger spare tire to be mounted onto the tailgate on a Jeep Wrangler JL. The tailgate hinges are upgraded from the stock die-cast aluminum castings to forged-steel hinge brackets. The kit includes a heavy-duty wheel mount that is fully adjustable for depth and tilt. Also included is an adjustable third brake light bracket. This system can handle tires sizes up to and including a 40-inch spare. No drilling is required for installation.

keep some large, heavy items outside the passenger compartment, which enhances safety.

Sport Cage

The rollover protection on the Gladiator JT and Wrangler JL is much stronger than the roll cage on the Wrangler JK. The Wrangler JL and Gladiator JT feature vertical A-pillar bars, which are much stronger. The steel alloy used in the roll cage is extremely tough. What is lacking is horizontal bracing above the dash and behind the top of the windshield. Rock Hard 4x4 offers a sport cage that addresses these issues. For extreme off-road terrain, the addition of sport cage add-on bars improves safety and adds rigidity to the body structure.

The Rock Hard 4x4 sport cage for the Gladiator increases body rigidity and improves safety by adding lateral and longitudinal bars to the existing roll-cage structure. Lateral tubes are installed just above the dash, across the top of the cockpit, above the front seats, and across the top at the rear of the cab. The longitudinal bars tie the lateral bars together for strength and safety. Installation is straightforward with the exception of drilling holes into the stock roll-cage structure, which is extremely hard. Rock Hard 4x4 includes special, high-speed drill bits to tackle the tough high-strength steel cage structure.

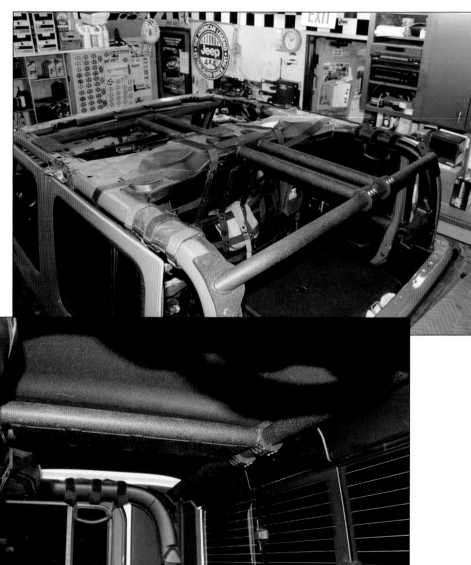

STYLING, ACCESSORIES, STORAGE, AND OVERLANDING UPGRADES

When the Jeep Wrangler JL first arrived, aftermarket parts were scarce. However, four model years into Wrangler JL production (and with the Gladiator JT added to the mix), the number of styling, storage, and accessory options has become overwhelming.

The Wrangler JK aftermarket offered more choices than any other vehicle in history, but the Wrangler JL and Gladiator JT surpass that record easily. In addition, with the exploding popularity of overlanding, even more product choices make decisions difficult and put a strain on the wallet.

Half and Tube Doors

A great feature of the Wrangler JL and Gladiator JT is the ability to easily remove the doors. The open-air feel is very appealing, especially off-road. With the doors removed, the visibility of the trail next to the Jeep improves also. The downside to doors-off driving is the increased vulnerability.

Half doors and tube doors provide a solution for increased secu-

rity while still offering the open-air feel. Some tube doors are strong and may offer improved side-impact protection when compared to stock doors. Many styles of tube and half doors are available from a wide range of companies. Rugged Ridge, DV8 Off-Road, Rough Country, Barricade, Steinjager, Bestop, Body Armor, Smit-

tybilt, Quadratec, and several other companies offer tube and half doors.

Stock Wrangler JL and Gladiator JT front door mirrors are not easy to remove. Most aftermarket tube doors have provisions for the mirror attachment. While tube doors are primarily used for off-roading, many vehicles drive on highways to the trails. Even

Styling and storage options for the Wrangler JL and Gladiator JT abound. With the ever-increasing popularity of overlanding, even more gear and accessory options make choices difficult. After all, JEEP is an acronym for "Just Empty Every Pocket!" (Photo Courtesy JP Molnar)

Doors-off four-wheeling is a great feature of the Wrangler and Gladiator. Tube doors from companies such as Rugged Ridge provide the open-air experience with an added measure of security and safety. The open-air experience gets a little chilly in the snow.

Rugged Ridge makes tube doors for the Wrangler JL, including the Fortis 1.5-inch diameter, black satin powder coat finish tube version. These doors have a very solid fit.

Moab is the perfect location to go topless and use tube doors, such as the High Rock 4x4 Element doors, for the Gladiator JT and Wrangler JL from Bestop. (Photo Courtesy Bestop)

off-road, having side mirrors adds to driving safety and is required by law in many cases. Many of the companies that offer tube doors also make mirror kits.

Bestop has been making Jeep soft tops for decades. The Bestop Trek Top Ultra features several options from full closure to full

Tops

In the tradition of the original Jeeps, the Wrangler JL and Gladiator JT can easily go topless. The soft tops are easy to open, and the hard tops can be removed. The Jeep aftermarket offers a myriad of replacement tops and some very functional and creative alternatives.

open. Bestop also makes fabric doors for the Wrangler JL and Gladiator JT. The two-piece fabric doors can be used with just the door section for more of an open-air experience or with the DOT-approved vinyl windows attached when the weather gets cold. This JL also features a Bestop Safari Bikini Top for some shade when the Trek Top is fully open. (Photo Courtesy Bestop)

The Bestop All-Weather Trail Covers provide interior protection when caught without a soft top. Door-opening protection flaps allow easy interior access when the cover is in place. (Photo Courtesy Bestop)

The Bestop Superior Ultra Top provides several options for open-air Jeeping, ranging from fully closed to fully open with its patented guide Track System. The top material is Bestop's premium twill fabric. (Photo Courtesy Bestop)

Soft-top options range from stock-replacement soft tops to elaborate designs. Some of the new tops operate like convertible tops from the 1950s and 1960s. Release a latch and slide the top back to a semi-open or to a fully open position. Soft tops are available in fully enclosed configurations as well as fastback designs.

Partial tops, sunshades, and half shades are also available for Wranglers and Gladiators. Color selections are limited for full tops, as are material choices. Sunshades and bikini tops are available in a wide range of colors to match exterior colors or to create contrasting, bright custom looks.

Bestop offers the Supertop Ultra, which has several configurations. It also offers several other soft top options. The Rugged Ridge Voyager soft top also offers several options for open-air driving. Other soft tops are offered by Mopar, RedRock Off-Road,

Jeeps have removable hardtops for the open-air experience. Removing the roof and doors is big job that requires two people and a good storage location. TopLift Pros makes a great mechanical lift system for removing the top from Wrangler JL two- and four-door models. The lever system provides quick top removal with one person and provides a convenient storage location. Attachments provide easy door removal and storage as well. TopLift Pros also offers a power attachment to make the job even easier. (Photo Courtesy TopLift Pros)

Rampage TrailView, JTopsUSA, Smittybilt, Rampage, and Steinjager.

Aftermarket options are limited for hardtops. DV8 Off-Road, Recon, and Guardian Fastback offer interesting alternatives to the stock Mopar hardtop.

Top-Removal Hoists

The hard top on the Wrangler JL Unlimited is heavy. The hard tops on the Gladiator JT and Wrangler JL two-door are a little lighter. In all cases, top removal is a two-person operation, but it is still awkward. Several companies make hard-top-removal hoists. Some are hand-crank powered, while others use an electric motor.

All hoists require a location to attach the lift securely. An outdoor structure or garage rafters are needed. Top Lift Pros offers a lever-style lift system that simplifies lifting the top and makes storage of the top convenient. An attachment for the Top Lift Pros system aids in removing the doors also.

Many Wrangler JLU owners opt to replace hardtops with the Bestop Superior Ultra Top. This premium soft top offers great versatility and high quality with excellent protection from the elements in all weather conditions. (Photo Courtesy Bestop)

Tuffy Security makes a wide range of lockable security solutions for the Gladiator JT and Wrangler JL. The Tuffy Laptop Portable Safe can be mounted securely under a seat and removed for portable use.

The Targa Sun Bikini Top from Bestop offers all-weather protection from the sun on the trail. Unlike some bikini tops, the Sun Targa does not interfere with hard or soft tops and requires no additional mounting channel. (Photo Courtesy Bestop)

Sunshades

Mesh sunshades provide protection from the sun while offering the open-air experience of going topless. Mesh sunshades can provide momentary protection from unexpected rain. Until a bump is encountered, that is. Then, occupants get

Rock Slide Engineering offers a tailgate-mounted folding table for the Wrangler JL. The Trail Tailgate Table is easy to install and made from lightweight powder-coated aluminum.

The Rock Slide Engineering Trail Tailgate Table folds out into a 20-inch-deep by 20-inch-wide table that is large enough for a Blackstone grill. The table even has a hook on the side to hang a trash bag.

doused with a cold shower. Several companies offer sunshades, including Rugged Ridge and SpiderWeb Shade.

Storage Options

Off-roading requires considerable amount of gear. Overlanding requires even more. Storage can be an issue. Gear, especially heavy items, needs secure storage that keeps items in place over rough terrain. Valuable

items need secure storage, especially when running topless and doorless.

Metal Storage and Security

Metal locking storage offers the best protection from theft and from heavy gear becoming dislodged over rough terrain or even in a crash. Tuffy Security Products offers a wide range of lockable, metal storage solutions for both the Gladiator JT and Wrangler JL. Storage containers are hard mounted and feature keyed locks.

Tuffy Security makes a Tailgate Lockbox for the Wrangler JL. The box holds a large amount of gear and is easily accessible. The steel construction can support up to 40 pounds.

Jeep provides a storage cubby under the floor of the rear cargo area in the Wrangler JL and JLU. Tuffy Security Products makes it easy for Jeep owners to upgrade to secure storage with its heavy-duty Locking Lid Cubby Cover for 2018–2021 Wrangler JL models. Providing concealed and theft-resistant lockable storage, the Locking Lid Cubby Cover protects tools and gear.

Tuffy Security's Tailgate Lockbox includes two trays for convenient storage. We chose to use the Tailgate Lockbox to store recovery gear because the tailgate location is so easily accessible. Almost any gear for camping, cooking, or other trail gear can be stored here. The fold-down lid works well as a work table. Installation is easy for two people.

Bolt Locks offers a Spare Tire Lock. The lock comes with a special wheel stud that replaces a stud in a spare-tire carrier. The lock works with a Gladiator JT or Wrangler JL key.

Just about anywhere there is space, Tuffy makes a storage solution.

Soft Storage

Soft storage bags offer excellent storage for lightweight and soft gear, such as recovery straps, clothing, and non-perishable food items. Many soft storage bags attach to the roll cage and fit in unused locations, such as the space between the rear windows and the roll-cage down tubes.

Other storage systems use a Molle

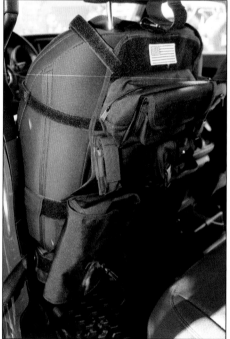

With modern on-board computers, batteries, and under-hood aftermarket accessories, such as cold air intakes, protecting under the hood is important. Bolt Locks makes a hood lock to provide that protection. Like other Bolt Locks, it operates with the Gladiator JT or Wrangler JL's key.

Rugged Ridge offers a Molle seat-back storage system. A seat-back panel straps to the seat. Several storage bags attach to the cover with Molle attachment points. A wide range of gear can be stored for quick, easy access.

Bolt Locks makes a wide range of locks using the key for the Jeep Gladiator JT and Wrangler JL. The Bolt Hitch Pin Lock keeps trailer hitches and shackle mounts from disappearing.

The rear cargo area in a Wrangler JL is subjected to much abuse, such as hauling heavy gear, wet items, spare or broken parts, and trash. Rugged Ridge makes a cargo floor liner to help protect the carpet from abuse.

front seat cover for storage behind the front seats. With the Molle system, many small bags can be used to store a variety of items for quick and easy access. Many companies manufacture soft storage solutions.

Locks

Padlocks are readily available from hardware stores. However, other types of locks protect vulnerable areas, including under-hood parts and the spare tire on Wrangler JLs. Bolt Lock makes a wide range of locks for Jeeps: hood locks, spare-tire locks, hitch-pin locks, trailer-hitch locks, cable locks, and padlocks. The unique feature of the Bolt Lock lineup is that all of the locks are programmed to work with your Jeep ignition key.

Floor Mats

Rubber floor mats that are molded to fit provide better protec-

Bestop's Ezroll soft tonneau cover for the Jeep Gladiator provides excellent protection from sun and weather while allowing quick, easy access to the bed for hauling. Installation requires no drilling due to a bolt-on clamp and bed rail system. (Photo Courtesy Bestop)

tion and much easier cleaning. Rear cargo floor liners are especially nice. Floor mats protect the carpet from damage. In addition, floor mats improve traction for the driver's and the passenger's feet in wet, snowy, or muddy conditions. Floor mats also add a customized look to the interior. Several companies produce floor mats, including Rugged Ridge, Mopar, and WeatherTech.

Roof Racks

Roof racks expand storage possibilities. Roof racks also provide

Rugged Ridge makes a complete set of floor mats for the Wrangler JL and Gladiator JT. The Rugged Ridge all-terrain floor liners are available for front and rear applications and fit perfectly.

The Rough Country roof rack system features built-in LED light mounts. The front of the rack fits a dual-row 50-inch bar, and the rear has accommodations for two 2-inch cube lights. The rack system is available with or without the lights. (Photo Courtesy Rough Country)

The Rough Country Jeep Gladiator low profile hard tri-fold tonneau cover locks into the tailgate when closed. The trifold design allows easy access, and the cover is easily removed. (Photo Courtesy Rough Country)

The Rugged Ridge AmFib snorkel system keeps water and dust from entering the engine's cold-air intake. The snorkel fits both the Wrangler JL and Gladiator JT. A low-mount version at hood height is also available. (Photo Courtesy Rugged Ridge)

mounting options for rooftop tents and a wide range of gear, including lights, shovels, Hi-Lift jacks, and water and fuel containers. The downside to a roof rack is the increased center-of-gravity height. Storing heavy gear on the roof makes the vehicle less stable and more susceptible to a rollover in extreme off-road terrain.

To compensate for the reduced stability over ruts, bumps, and side slopes, keep the vehicle as level as possible by selecting good driving lines. Rack systems for the Gladiator include roof racks, bed racks, and slide-out racks for a variety of gear. Many of the Gladiator rack designs are innovative as well as useful.

In addition to protected storage in the bed, bed racks offer storage systems for jacks, recovery tools, bicycles, canoes, fluid storage, and rooftop tents. Many rack options are available from Rugged Ridge, Yakima, Thule, Rough Country, Rhino Rack, Exposed Racks, Warrior Products, ARB, and several others.

A way to add a custom touch to a Wrangler JL or Gladiator JT is with colorful custom seat covers. PRP Seats makes a wide range of bolt-in seats and seat-cover designs with several color options. (Photo Courtesy PRP Seats)

Snorkels

Snorkels raise the air intake to roof level or above the hood, and they are a must-have item to ford deep water. Snorkels also provide much cleaner air when wheeling in dust clouds in the desert and on dusty trails. Rugged Ridge, ARB, Mopar, Flowmaster, and others make snorkels for the Gladiator and Wrangler JL.

Seats and Seat Covers

The stock and optional seats in the Gladiator JT and Wrangler JL are comfortable. For more aggressive off-road driving, several companies offer aftermarket seats with improved lateral support. The addition of four- or five-point harnesses helps secure and protect occupants in rough conditions. Several companies offer aftermarket seats, including Sparco, Mastercraft, PRP Seats, and Corbeau.

PRP, Rough Country, Smittybilt, and others also offer a wide range of seat covers in a variety of colors and designs.

ProLine Wraps offers a selection of precut and printed vinyl wraps for the Gladiator JT and Wrangler JL. Wraps are a great way to customize the look of a Jeep.

Graphic Wraps and Touch-up Paint

Graphic wraps provide a great opportunity for exterior customization and increased protection for expensive paint. ProLine Wraps and other companies offer premade partial wraps that are easily applied by the consumer. If mountain or desert pinstriping damages the paint or tree limbs and big rocks scrape the bodywork, companies like Mopar and automotivetouchup.com offer

Rear license plates are a must in all states—even off-road in most cases. Mounting an oversized spare tire blocks the stock license plate holder, which is also susceptible to trail damage. Rugged Ridge makes a license-plate and third-brake-light holder that is adjustable for optimum clearance.

Winch installations make it tough to mount a front license plate out of harm's way. Tuffy Security makes a front license-plate holder that rotates up and out of the way when the winch is in use.

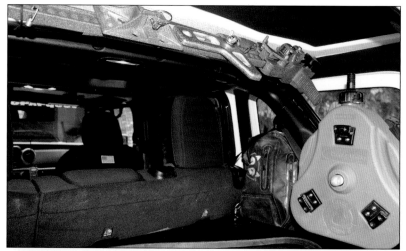

In addition to making great jacks for off-road use, Hi-Lift makes a really useful jack mount that attaches to the roll-cage crossbar in the cargo area of a Wrangler JL. An option to the jack mount is the Hi-Lift Trail Trak roll cage track mounting system for 2018–2021 Jeep Wrangler JL Unlimited. The jack mount uses nutserts, so holes must be drilled into the steel roll cage. A template is included. The drilling is the tough part. The roll cage in the JL seems to be made of kryptonite. Rock Hard 4x4 sells a drill bit kit for installing its sport cages. The kit contains two 1/4-inch cobalt hardened drill bits and a conical-tree die grinder. They work well.

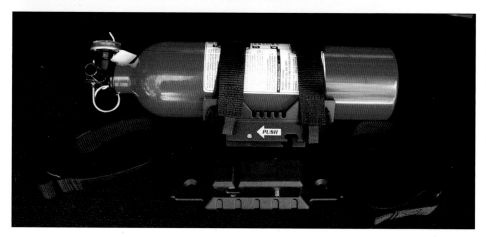

Fire extinguishers are a must-have item in a Jeep. Getting to them quickly and removing them easily for action is also critical. Rugged Ridge makes the Elite Fire Extinguisher Holder. The spring-loaded mount allows quick, one-handed removal in emergencies.

Overlanding

Overlanding, expedition travel, or backcountry adventure camping has been popular for decades. Today, the popularity of overlanding is significantly increasing. Overlanding

touch-up paint to match your Jeep.

Automotivetouchup.com provides complete kits for color-matching your exact paint code. Kits include primer, color paint, and clear coat. Both small-brush touch-up paint and spray cans are available. Kits include paint, sandpaper, tack cloths, and everything that is needed to complete a professional touch-up project.

Other Accessories

The Jeep aftermarket offers many additional accessories that range from brake-light relocation kits to fluid storage containers. Fire extinguisher holders, grab handles, jack mounts, license-plate holders, and a variety of mounts for radios and GPSs are available from many sources.

With the increasing popularity of overlanding, many companies are making products for the Gladiator, a perfect rig for overlanding adventures. Rooftop tents, racks with multiple mounts for a variety of gear, and truck bed storage are all popular overlanding gear options. (Photo Courtesy Henry Valesquez)

Off-road trailers, such as the Opus Lite, provide great off-road capabilities, comfort, and the option to leave the trailer at camp when exploring rugged terrain. (Photo Courtesy JP Molnar)

The Opus Lite off-road trailer uses a pop-up tent with many more comfort and utility options than a rooftop or rack-mounted tent. The Opus Lite uses a compressed-air inflation system to raise the tent when the trailer is opened and ready for setup. The process takes 90 seconds to complete. An exterior kitchen includes storage for cooking gear. (Photo Courtesy JP Molnar)

offers a great way to explore and is very family friendly. We will touch on overlanding gear here, but the topic is so broad that an entire book would barely scratch the surface.

Tents

For decades, a tent was the shelter of choice for vehicle-based travel and camping. Modern pop-up tents that require only a few seconds to deploy and stow are common. Dozens of companies make these tents. Other popular tents attach to vehicles, by either using the bed of a Gladiator or the back of a Wrangler as a sleeping area.

One of the concerns about ground tents is a wild animal attack. Attacks on humans are extremely rare. Attacks are even more rare on humans in tents. A rollover accident is much more likely with heavy gear or rooftop tents on top of a Wrangler JL or a Gladiator JT.

Rooftop Tents

Rooftop tents have significantly grown in popularity in the last decade. Many designs from a multitude of manufacturers are available. The common denominator among rooftop tests is the necessity of climbing a ladder for ingress and egress.

The only real drawback is the increased center of gravity height, which can cause instability in rugged terrain and additional wind resistance.

Off-Road Trailers

Off-road trailers offer many advantages for overlanding adventures: additional storage, improved stability, and the option to disconnect the trailer while exploring a local area. The cost is a disadvantage.

Off-road trailers are available in three basic configurations: small trailers with a rooftop tent on a rack, soft-sided pop-up styles, and hard-sided trailers.

Hard-sided trailers offer more privacy and improved comfort and protection. Some campgrounds do not allow soft-side tents or trailers. Many companies in the United States and Australia manufacture a wide variety of off-road trailers in different configurations, sizes, and floor plans.

The Opus Lite trailer sleeps two comfortably and features a removable table. The trailer weighs only 2,380 pounds dry. (Photo Courtesy JP Molnar)

Independent suspension and off-road tires allow the Opus Lite to traverse extreme terrain with good clearance and articulation. (Photo Courtesy JP Molnar)

One of the great joys of off-roading and overlanding is experiencing nature's scenery and serenity. An off-road trailer bridges the gap between roughing it and finding lodging for an extended trip. (Photo Courtesy JP Molnar)

Utility racks for the Gladiator provide a multitude of gear-carrying options. Exterior mounts for Rotopax extraction boards and awnings are available on many bed racks. An interior mount holds a propane tank. (Photo Courtesy Henry Valesquez)

Coolers and Refrigerators

Perishable food and cold beverages are mainstays of overlanding and day trips as well. Cold storage is a requirement for any off-road adventure. The most common cold-storage source is the traditional hard-shell cooler packed with ice or freezer ice packs. Soft-shell coolers, such as the AO Coolers Original Soft Cooler with high-density insulation, are becoming more popular. We have used the Arctic Ice Cooler Ice Packs in place of ice for several years. They last for a few days, depending on ambient temperatures.

Refrigerator/freezer units are pretty much required for extended overlanding trips. Several companies manufacture 12-volt plug-in refrigerators, and most of them have 110-volt power supplies. Some also offer freezer capabilities. We have been using the Type S Blizzard Box for about a year with great results.

Refrigerators come in several sizes and capacities. Prices range from about $400 to $1,500. ARB, Dometic, and Rough Country are popular brands for overlanding.

Electric refrigerators offer many more options for extended overlanding adventures and off-road day trips. The Type S Blizzard Box portable fridge and freezer operates on 12-volt vehicle power or from a 110-volt adapter when shore power is available. (Photo Courtesy Casey Sisson)

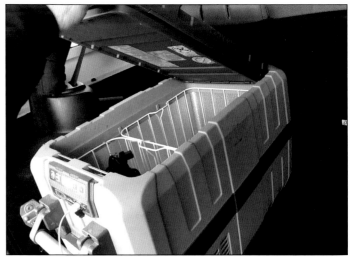

The Type S Blizzard Box lid opens from either end and is removable, exposing a roomy storage compartment with two removable baskets. The digital controls are easy to access. An interior light helps find food items in the dark. The vehicle battery is protected by a low-voltage cutoff. The control panel even features a USB charging port. (Photo Courtesy Casey Sisson)

STOCK ENGINES, UPGRADES, AND SWAPS

When Jeep launched the Wrangler JK in 2007, only one engine option was available: the 3.8L V-6. In 2012, the Wrangler was available with one engine: the Pentastar 3.6L V-6.

With the Wrangler JL, there are now five engine options, and there are two engine options for the Gladiator JT. The 3.6L Pentastar V-6 Engine Start/Stop (ESS) is still the standard engine for both the Wrangler and Gladiator. The 3.0L turbo diesel is an option for both.

The 3.6L Pentastar eTorque mild hybrid as well as a 2.0L turbo gasoline engine with ESS are also available for the Wrangler JL. However, the most exciting new engine option for the Wrangler JL is the 392-ci Hemi. The 6.4L Hemi produces a neck-snapping 470 hp and 470 ft-lbs of torque. The stock JL goes from 0–60 in about 4.5 seconds.

These engine choices will impact the Jeep aftermarket, especially the V-8 engine swap segment. While the additional cost of the factory Hemi option will likely be less than a Hemi engine swap, the difference will be small. Official pricing was not released prior to the publication of this book. For those with a pre-2021 Wrangler JL or any Gladiator JT, an engine swap is still a good option.

The introduction of the 392 Hemi in the Wrangler JL is a game changer for Jeep enthusiasts and will affect the Jeep aftermarket, especially the engine-swap market. The Hemi engine is a 392-ci 6.4L V-8 that produces 470 hp and 470 ft-lbs of torque. Jeep indicated that the Rubicon 392 accelerates from 0 to 60 mph in less than 4.5 seconds and rips through the quarter mile in 13 seconds. (Photo Courtesy FCA US LLC)

The drivetrain for the Rubicon 392 Hemi is identical to the standard Rubicon models. (Photo Courtesy FCA US LLC)

The 3.0L EcoDiesel V-6 engine available in the Gladiator JT and Wrangler JL offers 260 hp and 442 ft-lbs of torque. Towing capacity is a strong 3,500 pounds. Fuel economy is 29 mpg highway and 22 mpg city. The 3.0L EcoDiesel V-6 engine in the Gladiator JT and Wrangler JL uses the same drivetrain as other Wrangler and Gladiator models. (Photo Courtesy FCA US LLC)

The turbocharged 2.0L inline 4-cylinder engine produces 270 hp and 295 ft-lbs of torque with or without the belt-driven motor/generator. The belt starter/generator assists start/stop performance and low-speed acceleration. The 2.0L turbo is something of a hybrid with auxiliary power for the start/stop feature. Fuel economy is good. The turbo gas engine is not at its best in extreme off-road situations. (Photo Courtesy FCA US LLC)

The turbocharged 2.0L inline 4-cylinder engine is available in most Wrangler models using the same transmissions, transfer cases, and axles as with other engines. (Photo Courtesy FCA US LLC)

While the turbocharged 2.0L engine is more compact, the accessories take up considerable space. The driveline, axle, and transmission layout is the same for all Wrangler models. (Photo Courtesy FCA US LLC)

The Banks Ram-Air Intake System for the Jeep Wrangler JL and Gladiator JT 3.6L engine increases airflow by 82 percent over the stock air intakes. Intake air temperatures are also reduced. The Ram Air is available with either an oiled or a dry air filter. (Photo Courtesy Banks Power)

The Borla Climber Series catback exhaust system improves exhaust flow on the Wrangler JL 3.6L V-6 engine. Small horsepower increases can be expected from the stainless-steel exhaust system. The exhaust tone is throaty but not overly loud. The muffler is located between the frame rails in a much less vulnerable position.

Upgrades

Three of the Wrangler JL engine options have aftermarket-engine performance upgrades. Cold-air intakes and catback exhaust systems are available for the two versions of the 3.6L Pentastar and the 2.0L turbo gasoline engine. The cold-air intakes and the catback exhaust systems add small power increases and are relatively easy to install. Banks Power, aFe Power, Rough Country, K&N Filters, and several other companies offer cold-air intakes. Borla Exhaust, aFe Power, Magnaflow, Flowmaster, MBRP, and others offer exhaust systems for the Wrangler JL and Gladiator JT.

Engine tuning programmers can change the factory tune for the engine and add some power. The problem on the Wrangler JL and Gladiator JT is the locked powertrain control module (PCM). Complete

The Rough Country Jeep dual-outlet performance exhaust adds a more aggressive look to the back of a Wrangler JL and JLU. (Photo Courtesy Rough Country)

JBA Exhaust has developed a line of performance exhausts for the Jeeps. The JBA Wrangler JL exhaust replaces the stock muffler and a twin-tip tailpipe. The Gladiator JT muffler replaces the stock muffler and tailpipe in the stock location. The exhaust noise level is only slightly higher than stock but features a throaty exhaust tone.

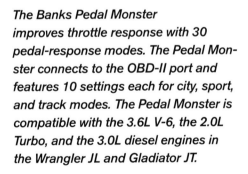

The Banks Pedal Monster improves throttle response with 30 pedal-response modes. The Pedal Monster connects to the OBD-II port and features 10 settings each for city, sport, and track modes. The Pedal Monster is compatible with the 3.6L V-6, the 2.0L Turbo, and the 3.0L diesel engines in the Wrangler JL and Gladiator JT.

The Banks iDash 1.8 DataMonster and SuperGauge for all 2008-plus OBD-II CAN bus vehicles, stand-alone instrument works on the 3.6L Pcn tastar V-6 engines in the Wrangler JL and Gladiator JT. The DataMonster can be programmed to read almost any engine data.

The Diablosport-PKITJL363019-i3-i3 and i3 Performance Tuner Combo includes a modified PCM for the 3.6L Pentastar engine. The stock PCM cannot be modified or tuned. With the DiabloSport package, many engine parameters can be tuned to improve performance and mileage as well as to monitor engine parameters.

tuning options require the use of a new PCM that must be programmed to be tuned externally.

DiabloSport and Superchips are two of the companies that make modified PCMs. Other tuners can help improve items such as throttle response, including the Banks Power Pedal Monster. More tuning products will become available as the aftermarket technology overcomes the restrictions on the computers and electronics on stock Wranglers and Gladiators.

Be aware that changing the tune on a factory computer may affect the vehicle warranty. Various FCA dealers treat warranty issues differently. Any modified part will not be covered under warranty. Modified components, such as the PCM, may be blamed for the failure of other parts. Plug-in modules, such as the Taser Mini and Superchips FlashCal do not affect the engine tune. They only affect items such as tire

The Vaitrix Booster ECU for the Jeep Wrangler JL 2.0 4-cylinder turbo is an advanced piggyback module that offers full boost control and curve control via RPM, as well as complete three-dimentional methanol injection programming.

size and gear ratio. They may not be an issue for warranties. They can also be easily removed before going to the dealership.

Forced Induction

Forced induction (superchargers and turbochargers) are a great way to increase power for considerably less money than an engine swap. Superchargers are available for the Pentastar 3.6L V-6 engine. Turbo boost systems are available for the 2.0L inline four turbo gas engine. Both are effective ways to increase power.

Currently, only one manufacturer offers a supercharger for the 3.6L Pentastar engine. The Edelbrock E-Force supercharger increases horsepower by about 20 percent and torque by 32 percent. The Edelbrock E-Force supercharger power gains are impressive, producing up to 309 hp and 289 ft-lbs of torque at the rear wheels. To date, Edlebrock produces the only supercharger available that works effectively with the locked PCM that is found in the Gladiator JT and Wrangler JL, and it is the only supercharger that achieved a 50-state emissions certification for the Pentastar engine.

V-8 Swaps

Engine swaps are still popular for Jeep Wranglers and Gladiators. However, the real need for more power makes swaps a little less desirable. The 850RE 8-speed automatic transmission and the D478 6-speed manual transmission gear ratios are game changers that negate the need for heavy horsepower increases. Acceleration improvements have been substantial. The launch of the 392 Hemi in the JL in 2021 also reduces the need for swapped V-8 power. For earlier Wrangler JLs and Gladiator JTs, V-8 swaps offer a viable alternative for upgrading power.

There are two popular engine swaps for the Wrangler JL and Gladiator JT: the Chrysler Hemi and a General Motors LS small-block Chevy derivative. The Hemi swap simplifies the process because the computer and the wiring are more compatible. The computer and the 850RE transmission can be used from the Wrangler JL/Gladiator JT. The ZF 8HP75 8-speed transmission is also used in LS V-8 engine swaps. The GM LS engine swap is more

While Hemi engine swaps may be a thing of the past with the advent of the 392 Hemi option in the Wrangler JL, Hemi swaps are still desirable in earlier JLs. This America's Most Wanted 4x4 Hemi 6.4L swap package was installed in Kevin and Brittany Williams' Stepchild 2018 Wrangler JL by DCD Customs in Chatsworth, California. Kevin and Brittany tackle some outrageous waterfalls and rocks in their legendary JL on their LiteBrite YouTube channel.

The Edelbrock Supercharger works on the 2018–2020 Jeep Wrangler JL/Gladiator JT with the 3.6L Pentastar V-6 engine. This is the only 50-state emissions-legal supercharger, and it fits under the factory hood with no modifications. It is not compatible with eTorque Hybrid models. (Photo Courtesy Edlebrock)

involved due to the need to change computer systems.

The installation of a V-8 in a Wrangler JL or a Gladiator JT is a major undertaking. Removal of the entire body from the frame make the swap easier. Engine swaps in older Jeeps, such as the CJ, were relatively easier. With each new Wrangler model and computerization, swaps have become increasingly more difficult and costly. The only viable option for a skilled home mechanic is the use of a complete coordinated package. Such kits start in the $20,000-plus price range. Turnkey installations can cost more than $80,000 for the extreme Hellcat and supercharged-LS swaps.

Hemi conversion kits are manufactured by America's Most Wanted 4x4, Savvy Off-Road, Mopar, and Dakota Customs. Several shops around the United States will perform the swap, including DCD Customs in Los Angeles. Several companies around the country will do the complete installation. On the GM LS side, MoTech, Bruiser Conversions, and RPM Extreme offer conversion kits and complete installation.

ELECTRICAL UPGRADES AND LIGHTS

Jeep Wrangler JLs and Gladiator JTs use several on-board computers to control just about everything. Adding electrical components by tapping into existing wires can damage the computers. Jeep offers a heavy-duty electrical group with auxiliary switches as standard equipment on some models, and it is available as an option on other models. The optional package is more costly than some of the aftermarket switching solutions.

Auxiliary Switch Solutions

The Jeep's heavy-duty electrical group includes four auxiliary switches. Overlanders and more serious off-roaders will most likely need more auxiliary switches for lights, radio communications, compressors, and lockers. Several auxiliary-switch options are available from the aftermarket.

A company called sPOD was among the first to offer switching solutions for the Jeep Wrangler. Its product line has grown, and the company now offers the eight-switch Bantam with highly sophisticated programming and smartphone apps. Several other companies offer a variety of switch panels.

The electrical system and electronics on the Wrangler JL and Gladiator JT are considerable. Add aftermarket components, such as air compressors, refrigerators, and auxiliary lights, and the demands are extreme. The auto shutoff start/stop feature used on Jeeps requires a small auxiliary battery to ensure the continuous operation of the electronics.

Auxiliary switches allow the stock wiring harness to be bypassed to protect the valuable computers from damage. Rough County offers the MLC-6 multiple light controller to operate electrical components directly from the battery through a terminal block with relays and fuses. Two dash-mounted switch panel options are available: a dash top mount or an in-dash panel allow for customization of the switch location.

The Rubicon models are equipped with a standard set of four auxiliary switches. The package is an option on other models. These switches can be used for lights or other electrical components. Most owners find four switches to be inadequate.

The terminal block control box on the MLC-6 multiple light controller mounts on a provided bracket in the engine compartment. An access cover protects the electronics and is easily removed. Six components can be operated with the MLC-6 multiple light controller. We run three sets of lights, front and rear lockers, and the on-board compressor.

The sPOD Bantam operates up to eight electrical components directly with a switch panel or a custom app for use with a smartphone.

The sPOD Bantam can be equipped with an optional touch screen switch panel. The touch screen allows many mounting options. The sPOD Bantam comes with many features and options for customization.

At the other end of the price spectrum is the Rough Country MLC-6 multiple light controller. The MLC-6 features six switches and two interior mounting options. The layout is similar to the original sPOD six-switch panel. All of the switching products share a direct connection to the vehicle battery to a control module. Auxiliary electrical components, such as lights, wire into the control module. A wiring harness runs to the switch panel that is mounted in the interior of the Jeep.

Auxiliary Lighting

As with many automotive electronic and electrical products, the lighting market has evolved with some very sophisticated lighting products that are nearly all LED–based in today's market. Even Jeep now offers a nice LED lighting package as an option on all Wrangler JLs and Gladiator JTs. For those not opting for Jeep's LED lighting option, many companies, including Mopar, offer LED lighting packages that vary in price considerably.

The Jeep LED package includes LED headlights and taillights. LED fog lights and daytime running lights are available on some models. Lower-price Wrangler JLs and Gladiator JTs can be equipped with a similar LED package that includes only the headlights and fog lights. Costs range from $900 to $1,600. Premium LED lights are available

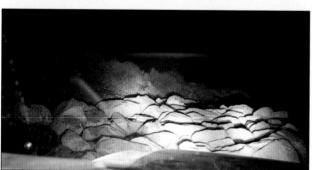

Wheeling in extreme terrain at night requires great lighting. A full array of Ultra Vision lights illuminate the Gold Mountain gatekeeper. The auxiliary lights are so bright that you cannot see the stock headlights.

From inside the Wrangler JL, the Ultra Vision lights turn night into light.

The Ultras Vision NITRO Maxx 105-watt 13-inch LED light bar produces more than 12,000 lumens. This light bar also has high- and low-beam functions.

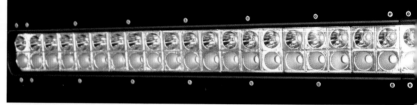

The Type S app-controlled 24-inch smart light bar provides control from your smartphone. Light output exceeds 18,000 lumens. While this light bar is powered from the vehicle battery, no switch wiring is necessary. The lights are completely controlled from the smartphone app.

from many aftermarket resources less expensively.

While the factory LED light option works well, additional auxiliary lights improve visibility at night, especially on difficult trails. The latest LED lights can be programmed to create a variety of lighting effects and even light shows. Some lights operate using smartphone apps.

Auxiliary lights are available in several designs that range from light bars of different sizes to driving lights, cube A-pillar-mount lights, fog lights, flush-mount lights, and rock lights. All are available in a variety of lighting patterns that range from narrow, long range to wide. Some light bars use LEDs of different light patterns so that you receive the benefits of both wide and narrow patterns. High- and low-beam functions are also found on some lights.

Light Bars

Light bars, especially the large 48-inch roof-mount type, can put out tremendous amounts of light. Smaller light bars can be mounted on the hood or bumper. Roof-mount light bars have several issues. The first is reflection off the hood. This can be distracting. Wind noise is another issue. Light-bar covers can help reduce wind noise.

Some states have laws that limit the height of light bars (or any auxiliary lighting) to at or below the level of the headlights. Some states allow the light bar to be covered when operating on the highway or streets.

The Ultra Vision NITRO Maxx 155-watt 18-inch LED light bar puts out over 18,000 lumens. The light bar has a high-beam function that uses all 57,00K-temperature LEDs. The low-beam function uses only the spread optics with warmer 4,000K LEDs, which reduces glare on road signs and fog.

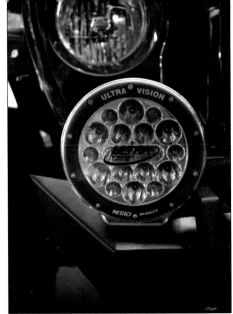

The project JL was not equipped with the factory LED light package. The stock head-lights are completely inadequate for serious night driving on the trails. We equipped the JL with a lighting package from Ultra Vision that includes round driving lights, fog lights, an 18-inch light bar, and cowl-mounted light cubes. Night vision is not an issue.

The Ultra Vision NITRO 80 Maxx LED driving light uses 19 LEDs, which put out more than 8,000 lumens of light. The Nitro 80 Maxx driving lights come with a mount that is perfect for bum-pers. All Nitro lights come complete with an easy-adjust mounting bracket, clear lens covers, a wiring harness, and anti-theft nuts.

Rough Country offers a selection of LED light bars. The 50-inch windshield light bar is available with either single- or double-row lights. The hood-mount light bar mounts to the cowl. The Rough Country bumper comes with a pair of flush-mount LED cube lights and a bumper hoop. The bull bar features an integrated single-row 20-inch LED light bar.

Fog lights can assist a spotter at night, unlike light bars, driving lights, and LED headlights, which can blind a spotter. Wrangler JLs and Gladia-tor JTs come with fog lights. Several companies offer replacement fog lights with superior illumination. The Ultra Vision Nitro smart driving light fits in the stock fog light receptacle. This light features both low- and high-beam settings, turn-signal func-tion, and a ring light with adjustable color setting.

Driving Lights

An advantage to driving lights is the compact size, which allows them to be mounted to bumpers. A pair of bumper-mounted driving lights can be angled outward slightly to improve coverage. Driving lights are available in various lighting patterns and light temperatures.

Fog Lights

Several companies offer fog lights that fit in the stock fog-light recep-tacles. Many aftermarket bumpers feature openings and mounts for stock or aftermarket replacement fog lights.

Cube Cowl Lights

Cowl lights can also be angled outward, usually at a greater angle than driving lights to help illuminate the sides of a trail. This is especially helpful when navigating tight turns that are lined with obstacles. Several companies offer a wide range of cube lights and cowl mounts for the Wrangler JL and Gladiator JT.

Rock Lights

Rock lights were seen as a mall-crawler fad when they were first introduced. In reality, rock lights can be a great aid for rock crawling on night runs. The underside lights make it easy for a spotter to see obstacles under the Jeep. White-colored lights are the most effective.

Note that it is often best to minimize using really bright lights when a spotter is trying to see a rig. The bright lights can be blinding and may cause misdirection.

Daylight Driving on Dusty Trails

Dust can make trails visibility difficult during the day, especially to oncoming traffic. Run all lights during dusty conditions, even in daylight. In addition, when Jeeping in a group, unless you are the run

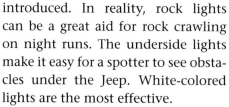

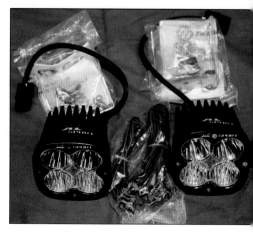

Baja Designs manufactures a complete line of high-end LED lights for off-road use. The cube-style lights work well as cowl lights or mounted to a winch bumper.

Seeing the edges of the trail in the dark requires good lighting. Cowl-mounted cube lights can be angled a few degrees outboard to light up the edges of the trail and make turning around tight corners easier. The Ultra Vision Atom 25-watt LED light produces 2,900 lumens from six LEDs.

The Rugged Ridge high/low-beam LED Cube Light Combo make excellent cowl-mounted lights.

Rugged Ridge makes a useful cowl-mounting bracket for the Wrangler JL and Gladiator JT. The cowl mounts work with any cube or round driving light.

If you are looking for something completely different to mount cowl lights on a Wrangler JL or Gladiator JT, the Rock Slide Engineering Cowl LED light pod brackets fit the bill. They are made from 3/16-inch steel and powder coated with a textured black finish. (Photo Courtesy Rock Slide Engineering)

Even the brightest LED lights will not penetrate thick dust to aid visibility for the driver. Running LED lights on dusty trails in the daylight does allow others to see you.

The Midland MicroMobile 15-watt GMRS two-way radio with an integrated control microphone has a 50-mile-range line of sight with an external-mount antenna. (Photo Courtesy Midland Radio)

leader, be careful when using auxiliary lights. The drivers in front can be easily blinded by bright lights from behind.

Auxiliary lights are available from many sources. Ultra Lights from Australia offers a wide range of light bars, driving lights, fog lights, and cube lights. American–based companies, such as Baja Designs, Rigid, JW Speaker, and KC HiLites all make premium lighting in a wide range of designs. Type S Automotive offers some innovative lights that can be operated and programmed with smartphone apps.

Radio Communications

Citizens band (CB) radios were the go-to form of radio communication for many years. In recent years, ham radios have become very popular. Dual-band (UHF and VHF) radios with ham and commercial channels offer more frequency choices, including non-ham channels that do not require a ham license.

Due to short range, CB radios are becoming much less popular. General Mobile Radio Service (GMRS) radios are rapidly gaining popularity, especially with Jeep clubs. GMRS radios operate on several different

General Mobile Radio Service (GMRS) radios are rapidly becoming the radio system of choice for Jeep events and clubs. GMRS radios require a license (no test, just a $70 fee for 10 years) to operate on GMRS frequencies, but GMRS radios also operate on Family Radio Service (FRS) frequencies that require no license. Midland Radios is on the leading edge of GMRS radio technology.

Rugged Radios offers a handheld dual-band ham and commercial radio. It also makes a nice dash mounting bracket for the handheld. Rugged Radios offers a wide selection of radios for Jeeps and all off-road applications.

frequency ranges, including the Family Radio Service (FRS) frequencies. GMRS radios require a license, but no test is involved as there is with a Ham radio license. A license costs $70 for 10 years. No license is needed to operate on the FRS frequencies.

Midland Radios is on the leading edge of GMRS radios with a 40-watt version that has a range of 40-mile line of sight. The Midland MXT400 is loaded with features, including 8 repeater channels and 15 high-power channels.

Satellite Messengers

Satellite messengers provide satellite communications via test message and emergency contacts with first responders. While it is always best to travel the backcountry in groups, the satellite messengers, such as the Garmin InReach and the SpotX, make solo travel much more viable.

GPS and GPS Apps

Aftermarket GPS systems and apps designed for off-road travel generally provide more accurate and

GPS apps for smartphones and tablets have increased in popularity, especially for the overlanding market. OnX, GAIA, and All Trails are just a few.

up-to-date information. The Magellan TRX7 GPS unit allows advanced trip planning and trip tracking. Several GPS apps use both iOS and Android operating systems for use on tablets and smartphones. GAIA, onX, and Alltrails are designed for backcountry use. As reliable as modern GPS systems are, carrying a paper map as a backup is highly advised.

The Z Automotive Tazer electronic calibration module is tiny. The module plugs into the OBDII port. The list of items the Tazer can calibrate or toggle on/off is impressive. Tire diameter, axle gear ratios, sway bar operation, and many other features fall under the Tazer's control.

Electronic Calibration Modules

Electronic calibration modules allow the vehicle's computer to be reprogrammed to change a wide range of parameters, including tire diameter, gear ratio, and transfer-case ratio. The go-to module for the Gladiator JT and Wrangler JL is the Tazer from Z Automotive. A long list of Jeep JL and Gladiator JT features can be disabled or enabled with the Tazer.

Batteries and Jumper Batteries

The addition of auxiliary lights, a winch, and other electronic devices puts a strain on the battery. Aftermarket batteries from Odyssey and Optima are designed to handle the additional electrical power requirements and rigors of off-road driving. Given the potential for battery overload or failure, carrying a jumper battery is a sound practice. Type S Automotive offers a very compact jump starter and power bank.

The Magellan TRX7 GPS provides thousands of off-road trail maps for the TRX7, including many crowd-sourced maps. You can also record trails you drive and save them for future use or share on the TRX7 website. Creating a route is easy on Magellan's TRX7 app.

Batteries take a beating when off-roading in a Wrangler JL or Gladiator JT. Odyssey makes a line of batteries designed for the extreme conditions of four-wheeling. We have had Odyssey batteries for several years, and they outlast the stock or OEM replacement batteries by two to three times.

The Type S 12-volt jump starter and 8,000-mAh portable power bank provide a compact source of battery power for jump-starting vehicles and charging both USB-A- and USB-C-port mobile devices. It even has an LCD that displays step-by-step jump-starting instructions.

All Jeep Wrangler JLs and Gladiator JTs use a small auxiliary battery to power the electronics when the auto start/ stop feature is engaged when the vehicle is at rest. The auxiliary battery is located under the main battery and fuse block. It is accessible through the passenger-side fender's inner liner. When these batteries lose charge or fail, it plays havoc with the electronics, and the dash readouts fail. Quinn's Gladiator needed a replacement auxiliary battery after 7,000 miles.

Most directions to remove the auxiliary battery suggest removing the main battery, the fuse block, and a bunch of wires. The auxiliary battery is much more easily accessed by removing the passenger-side inner fender liner and then removing the three bolts that hold the battery in place.

VEHICLE RECOVERY GEAR, WINCHES, AND TRAIL TOOLS

A variety of tools make recovering a stuck Jeep much easier. While winches are cool, other tools may work more effectively, depending on the circumstances. While a winch can be used in most cases, kinetic yanker straps, off-road jacks, and extraction boards may be easier and more effective.

TECH TIP
The Seven Most Important Recovery Tools

- Tow strap
- Shackles (soft shackles are best)
- Kinetic (yanker) strap
- Extraction boards
- Shovel
- Off-road jack
- Winch

Winching operations often occur in less-than-desirable conditions. (Photo Courtesy Rough Country)

Tow Strap

Tow straps work the best for towing, but they can also be used for pulling out a stuck vehicle. Recovering a stuck vehicle should be done with no slack in the strap (unlike a kinetic yanker strap). Tow straps have very little stretch or give. Use only tow straps with stitched-material loops on the ends. Metal hooks tend to break under higher loads. The most common straps are 20 to 30 feet long by 3 inches wide.

Shackles

Shackles are used for attaching winch line or tow straps to a vehicle. Shackles must be rated stronger than the strap or winch line to which they are attached. Two types of shackles are commonly used. The most common is the D-ring shackle that is made of high-strength steel. The soft shackle is becoming more popular. Soft shackles are made from the same synthetic materials that are used for synthetic winch line. If a D-ring shackle fails, it can cause damage or serious injury. Soft shackles are safer, easier to use, and lighter.

D-ring shackles, also called bow shackles, allow for the attachment of a winch line, tow strap, or recovery rope to a mount on a vehicle. The D-ring shackle must be rated for more strength than any other link in the recovery system. Most synthetic winch lines are rated at more than 20,000 pounds of strength. A shackle should be rated for more than 25,000 pounds. (Photo Courtesy Rough Country)

A synthetic shackle makes recovery connections easier. The shackle here is mounted to a Factor 55 rope retention recovery ring that replaces a snatch block in winching operations. The rope shackle is heavier than the winch line. (Photo Courtesy Factor 55)

Kinetic (Yanker) Strap

A kinetic strap functions like a large bungee cord. When it is stretched, it stores energy. Unlike a chain, a cable, or a nylon tow strap, which do not stretch much when a pulling force is applied, the kinetic strap is designed to store energy as it is stretched. Then, when it is snapped back, the effective pulling force increases because the strap snaps back faster than it was stretched.

Kinetic yanker straps are used to yank a stuck rig off an obstacle or out of mud, snow, or sand. The forces are substantial, even though the kinetic shock-absorption characteristics of the kinetic strap soften the blow. Attach the yanker strap with a shackle to a secure point on each rig.

Extraction Boards

Extraction boards are best used when a vehicle is stuck in soft surfaces, such as snow, mud, and sand. The lugs on the board are designed to engage with the tire tread. When the tires begin to rotate, the tire tread pulls on the lugs on the board. The boards then elevate the Jeep as it moves forward (or backward) and provide a solid surface to get unstuck. They are easy to use and often the quickest way to get unstuck. They do not work on hard surfaces or rocks.

Extraction boards, including the MaxTrax, use lugs on the platform for traction to pull and lift a stuck vehicle out of situations like deep snow. The ends of the boards are scooped and can be used to shovel under the tire to remove enough material to place the board for maximum performance.

Several companies make extraction boards, including Rough Country (shown here). (Photo Courtesy Rough Country)

Shovels

Shovels are most often used to dig out of snow when stuck, but they are not much help in sand or mud. They are also used for digging holes to place ground anchors for winching. Folding shovels are very inexpensive and compact. More useful options included multitool kits, such

Multiuse tool kits, such as the Max Axe, provide a compact solution for carrying trail work tools. The Max Axe handle uses a permanently mounted ax head on the handle with attachments that pin to the ax head. Attachments include a shovel, a rake, and various pick heads.

as the Hi-Lift Handle-All, which uses a telescoping handle and shovel, pick, sledge hammer, and ax head attachments. The Max Axe is a similar tool kit with interchangeable attachments.

Off-Road Jacks

Off-road jacks provide a means of changing a flat tire and gaining clearance under a tire when a vehicle is stuck. The Hi-Lift jack is the gold standard of off-road jacks. The Hi-Lift jack can be used in a variety of vehicle recovery situations as well as when changing tires. Hi-Lift offers many accessories as well. In recent years, many other off-road jacks have flooded the market. Many copy the Hi-Lift design, while others offer some innovative jacking solutions.

ARB offers a hydraulic hand-cranked vertical jack that is easy to use, expensive, and a little bulky. Pro Eagle makes a traditional-looking floor jack with off-road-type wheels and tires. This jack makes lifting a Jeep really easy, but the cost is high and storage can be an issue. While the vertical jacks work well for lifting, changing a tire is problematic due the distance the body/frame must be raised to get the tire free from the road surface.

Hi-Lift sells the Lift-Mate, which is designed to directly lift the vehicle from a wheel, which greatly reduces the amount of travel up the jack bar that is needed to lift the wheel off the ground. The Lift-Mate is also the quickest way to lift a vehicle that is high-centered on rocks, humps, or logs. Another option for tire changing is a compact, inexpensive bottle jack. A bottle jack can be placed under the axle housing near the offending tire to quickly lift the tire off the ground.

Winches

Winches usually provide the easiest way to get unstuck. With the ever-increasing popularity of Jeeps, off-roading in general, and overlanding, many companies have entered the winch market. It can be difficult to know which winch will get the job done safely and over the long haul. Quality is important. The last issue anyone wants is a winch failure during a critical recovery process.

We have seen several winches fail during our vehicle-recovery classes. The failure points are most often related to electrical wiring that shorts out. We recommend quality winches that we have used, including Warn, NovaWinch, Trekker from Rugged Ridge, Ramsey, and Viking. There are many economy brands also available.

For the more economical winches, we recommend using the winch at about half the maximum

The Hi-Lift jack has been around for more than 100 years and is nearly standard equipment for a Jeep. Hi-Lift makes a clean roll cage mount for the Wrangler JL. The mount holds the jack in place out of the way and in a much cleaner environment than when mounted outside. The mount also holds an optional attachment for other gear, such as a Power Tank or Daystar cam can fluid container.

The Rugged Ridge Trekker winch is mounted to a Rugged Ridge HD stubby bumper. The bumper features massive attachment points for shackles, notches for a Hi-Lift jack, pockets for stock fog lights, and the winch mount. The Trekker winch's maximum load is 9,500 pounds with a synthetic winch line and an aluminum Hawse fairlead.

The Warn Zeon 9500S winch uses a synthetic winch line, a Factor 55 Hawse fairlead, and a Factor 55 UltraHook winch hook with the shackle mount. The stubby winch bumper is from Casey Currie.

The Novawinch Pro 9500 electric winch is made by Symonds in the United States. While the name is fairly new in the winch market, the product has been available for several years under another brand name. The line speed with no load is 52.5 feet per minute and 4.3 feet per minute at a full 9,500-pound load. The gear box is a two-stage planetary/two-stage spur gear with a ratio of 171:1. The 12-volt, DC motor produces 6 hp.

Rough Country offers a Pro 9500S winch with synthetic winch line and a fully integrated stubby winch bumper with shackle mounts, flush lights, and a light bar. (Photo Courtesy Rough Country)

While the Novawinch name is new, the winch is not. Novawinch is the rebranded Superwinch Talon. This winch features 12,500 pounds of pulling power from a 6-hp motor. The line speed is a fast 50 feet per minute unloaded and 3.3 feet per minute fully loaded. The red switch key on the left of the bumper is an electrical cutoff switch for the winch. When it is not in use, the switch cuts power to the winch, which would protect the electrical system if the winch power cables would short out.

The Rugged Ridge Trekker S10 winch has plenty of pulling power to extract any Gladiator JT or Wrangler JL out of sticky situations. The 5.6-hp, series-wound motor transmits power through a three-stage planetary gearset with a 212:1 ratio.

The Novawinch uses a plug-in winch controller. Novawinch is now offering a wireless remote that plugs into the controller socket on the winch. Operational range is about 65 feet. We had to do a little trimming to the bottom of the grille to fit the winch on the Rugged Ridge bumper.

pull capacity. So, for a 10,000-pound economy winch, use a snatch block for any pull that is estimated to exceed 5,000 pounds. This will keep the load as light as possible to reduce strain on the winch.

Most Wrangler JLs and Gladiator JTs weigh around 5,000 to 7,000 pounds. The minimum winch pull rating should be 9,500 pounds, and a 12,500-pound pull rating is more desirable. Keep in mind that the load on the winch is more than just the vehicle weight. The terrain is a significant factor. A pull on a flat, level, hard surface requires only about 100 pounds. The power needed to pull up a 45-degree slope with a smooth, hard surface is equal to the weight of vehicle. If that surface happens to be deep sand, snow, or soft dirt, you can double the pulling power necessary.

With a 10,000-pound rated winch, add a snatch block pulley to double the pulling power of the winch. The maximum pulling power of a winch occurs when the winch line is nearly fully unspooled with only one layer around the winch spool. When the winch line is fully wound, most winch lines will have four layers around the spool. The least pulling power occurs when most layers of the winch line are on the spool. With four layers on the spool, pulling power is reduced nearly 50 percent (or about 12 percent per layer).

Winch Line:
Wire Rope versus Synthetic

Wire rope has a singular advantage: cost. Synthetic winch line is

The Factor 55 ProLink replaces a traditional hook at the end of the winch line. The Factor 55 ProLink creates a true closed winching system that is stronger and safer. The shackle-mounting hole can accommodate a soft shackle.

light and considerably safer. Synthetic line absorbs shock load better, which softens the abrupt loads as slack is taken up. The synthetic line is much easier to handle, especially when rewinding on the winch drum.

Wire rope strands can break and cause potential gashes on unprotected hands. Synthetic line will not cause cuts when it is frayed. Synthetic line is thicker for a given tensile strength, and the length of line on the winch spool is shorter than on wire cable.

Winch Controllers

Two types of winch controllers are commonly used. The most common is the plug-in remote, which attaches to the winch for operation. Remote winch controllers use a signal from a handheld controller to operate the winch. The advantage with the remote winch controller is the ability to use it away from the vehicle, out of harm's way. Be sure

The Novawinch 12.5 easily pulled our project JL up a deeply rutted 40-degree slope. The estimated load was about 8,000 pounds. Line speed was impressive.

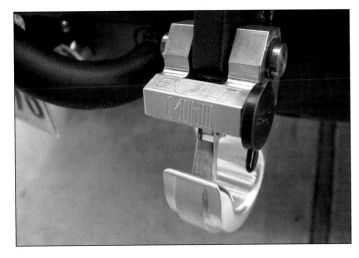

Bolt Locks makes a unique recovery hook for towing, winching, or other vehicle recovery operation. The massive recovery hook has one completely unique feature: it is lockable using your Jeep's key (as with other Bolt Lock products).

that the battery is working before heading on an off-road adventure.

Winching Accessories

Winch line end links connect the winch line to a strap or another vehicle. Most end links are hooks with a spring-loaded latch that retains the hook to its attachment point. Other end links accommodate closed-system winching rigging.

Closed-system winching features connections with no openings, including those found on hooks. A connection that uses a hook with sheet-metal spring-loaded safety latches is not a closed system. End links for closed-system winching are available in several designs. Factor 55 is a leader in winching closed-system recovery hardware. Closed-system winching rigging is much more secure and safer.

Winch fairleads help control the direction and smooth flow of the winch line when being spooled or unspooled. Two types of fairleads are used. The roller fairlead features four rollers around the perimeter of the fairlead mount and is used for wire rope winch line. A Hawse fairlead is generally made from machined aluminum with a smooth radius on the opening. Hawse fairleads are used with synthetic winch line.

Shackles are critical. Another critical accessory is the snatch block. A snatch block (or pulley) increases the pulling power of a winch. Snatch blocks can also alter the direction of the winch line if necessary when a straight-line pull is not possible.

A new style of snatch block that is called a retention ring or pulley is much lighter and easier to use compared to a traditional snatch block. Retention rings look like a metal wheel with a groove for the synthetic winch line and a smooth center bore for a soft shackle. The soft shackle anchors to a tree-saver strap or a second vehicle, and the winch line runs back to the winching vehicle to be attached to a shackle mount on a bumper.

Another important winching accessory is a tree-saver strap. A tree-saver strap is looped around a tree base to winch against. Wider straps are better because they spread the load across a larger area and reduce the risk of damaging the tree. Never loop a winch line (synthetic or steel) around a tree. When no natural attachment point is available to winch against, another vehicle can be used.

In some cases, either no other vehicle is available or it is impossible to get another vehicle positioned to assist in the winching operation. A ground anchor, such as a Pull Pal, comes into play in these situations. We have used the Pull Pal for years in these situations with great success in nearly any surface except rocks. You won't need one often, but when you do, the Pull Pal is game changer.

Other important winching accessories include gloves to protect the hands and a winch line damper. Winch line dampers keep a winch line from flying should the loaded line break. Dampers are important on any winch line, but they are critical on steel winch rope. Winch manufacturers offer both weighted dampers and dampers with pockets for weights, such as rocks or sand. An alternative to commercial winch line dampers is the use of a blanket, a towel, or a jacket on the winch line when the line is under load.

The traditional-style snatch block from ARB is rated at 30,000 pounds. The pulley is sandwiched between two rotating brackets that allows the winch line to be inserted. A shackle connects to the brackets holding the winch line in the snatch block.

A tree-saver strap protects the tree bark from damage. Wider straps spread the load over a greater area, which further reduces the possible damage. The tree-saver strap is attached to a 7P recovery ring for a winching recovery operation.

The standard Pull Pal uses a solid spade. An optional dimpled spade is available. The dimpled spade is much lighter with no loss in pulling power. The Pull Pal works in soft surfaces, such as mud, sand, and snow. It also works well in hard dirt surfaces. It is not designed for use in large rocks. We have used the Pull Pal in many conditions; it is always a bit of a surprise when the spade digs in and the winch starts to pull the vehicle. (Photo Courtesy Pull Pal)

The Factor 55 rope retention pulley replaces a snatch block for winching use. A soft shackle is used in the pulley center for both attachment and rotation when the winch is in use. A unique feature of the Factor 55 rope retention pulley is the series of rubber studs that help hold the synthetic winch line in place when the line is not under tension. (Photo Courtesy Factor 55)

The Pull Pal ground anchor creates a winching pull point when trees, other vehicles, or other winching points are not available. The spade attachment is designed to be pulled into the ground with the winch. The winch line attaches to the mounting hole on the end of the scissor-arm assembly. This Pull Pal is rated for 11,000 pounds.

JEEP PROJECTS

The projects in this chapter feature Don's 2020 Wrangler JL Unlimited Sport S and Quinn's All J Products 2020 Jeep Gladiator JT Rubicon.

The authors built new Jeeps while working on this book project. Quinn's Gladiator JT Rubicon is on the left. Don's Wrangler JL Sport is on the right. Both rigs are daily drivers but also see some extreme trail use, including the challenging Cake Walk trail in Cougar Buttes, which is part of the King of the Hammers race course. (Photo Courtesy Toby Jho)

Don Alexander: 2020 Jeep Wrangler JL Unlimited Sport S

When selecting a Wrangler JL model, we decided to go with the Sport S Unlimited instead of a Rubicon for a few reasons. First, most of the equipment on the Rubicon, such as the Dana 44 axles, power steering, and suspension, were being replaced. Second, the price was more than $10,000 less.

While the JL project is used mostly as a daily driver, it is also used for testing and for the Trails 411 YouTube channel video shoots. In addition, we wanted to be able to use 40-inch-diameter tires, so the emphasis was more on being a trail rig.

The Rubicon transfer case was the only item that made the Rubicon a solid choice. The 4.0:1 low-range ratio in the Rubicon is desirable compared to the 2.72:1 low-range ratio in the Sport S. The 8-speed automatic transmission with a very low first-gear ratio made the decision to go with the Sport model much easier. The crawl ratio, even with 40-inch tires, is more than adequate due to the low first-gear ratio in the 8-speed automatic.

Axle articulation exceeded expectations with the RockJock 4-inch pro lift, AntiRock off-road sway bars, and the Bilstein B8 8100 bypass shock absorbers. (Photo Courtesy Toby Jho)

Steep rock climbs, such as Chicken Rock in Cougar Buttes, are almost too easy with the 40-inch Mickey Thompson Baja Boss tires and the 5.38 Yukon gears in the Currie 60 Extreme axle assemblies. (Photo Courtesy Toby Jho)

Driving V-notches requires stability, good traction, and good brakes. (Photo Courtesy Toby Jho)

Even with the 2.72:1 low-range transfer case in the JL Sport S, steep descents are not an issue with the Yukon 5.38:1 gears and the big brakes on the Currie 60 Extreme axles. (Photo Courtesy Toby Jho)

Tire flex is needed to climb undercut rocks. The Mickey Thompson Baja Boss 40s on Raceline Monster bead-locks provide the flex. The RockJock Suspension allows plenty of flex, and the Rugged Ridge HD fenders provide good clearance for the big tires. (Photo Courtesy Toby Jho)

Quinn Thomas: All J Products 2020 Jeep Gladiator JT Rubicon

Quinn had his eyes on a Gladiator JT ever since it was announced. He purchased it during the 2019 SEMA Show in Las Vegas, Nevada. That was about the same time that we agreed to write this book. Quinn decided to build the All J Gladiator in phases, starting with 35-inch-diameter tires on a 2-inch Daystar spacer lift.

He tested the Gladiator on some black-diamond trails, including Gold Mountain, a Jeep Badge of Honor trail in Big Bear Lake, California. Quinn and the Gladiator handled the trails with ease. The fears about breakover and departure angles proved minimal.

The final phase of the build (so far—because Jeep builds are never complete) included upgrades to Rockjock suspension and AntiRock sway bars, Fox bypass shocks, PSC power steering, Artec belly pan skids, and Genright fenders. These upgrades were performed to accommodate the Nexen Roadian MTX mud-terrain tires.

Quinn also used Artec trusses on the stock axle housings to improve strength on the extreme trails. Yukon Gear 5.13:1–ratio ring and pinions replaced the stock 4.10:1 gears in the stock housings, retaining the stock electric lockers. Several other modifications have made Quinn's daily driver into a very capable trail and rock-crawling machine.

Quinn's Gladiator has considerable flex with the aid of the RockJock lift and Fox bypass shocks. (Photo Courtesy Toby Jho)

The Nexen Roadian MTX mud-terrain tires provide plenty of traction on the wet black-diamond trail Holcomb Creek, which is a Jeep Badge of Honor trail in Big Bear Lake. (Photo Courtesy Toby Jho)

The stock steering left a lot to be desired on the big rocks. Steering was extremely difficult in tight quarters. Quinn installed the PSC power steering system shortly after this run. Problem solved. (Photo Courtesy Toby Jho)

The Gladiator initially had a bad rap for performance in the rocks. Quinn has proven otherwise with the rock-crawling capabilities of his All J Products Gladiator JT Rubicon. (Photo Courtesy Toby Jho)

The first phase of Quinn's All J Products Gladiator JT build used 35-inch Nexen Roadian MTX tires on Raceline wheels. A 2-inch Daystar spacer lift provided plenty of tire clearance with stock fenders.

PROJECT JEEP SPECIFICATIONS

Don Alexander's 2020 Jeep Wrangler JL Unlimited Sport S

Year/Model	2020 Wrangler Sport S Unlimited
Engine	Stock
Transmission	Stock
Transfer case	Stock 2.72:1
Tires	37 inch x 12.50 inch x 17 inch Nexen Roadian MTX; 40 inch x 13.50 inch x 17 inch Mickey Thompson Baja Boss
Wheels	Raceline Boost 17 x 9, 8 x 6.5; Raceline Monster Beadlock 17 x 9, 8 x 6.5
Rear axle housing	Currie 60 Extreme
Front axle housing	Currie 60 Extreme
Rear ring and pinion	Yukon Gear 5.38
Front ring and pinion	Yukon Gear 5.38
Rear axles	Currie chrome-moly 40-spline full floating
Front axles	Currie chrome-moly 1-ton 35-spline inner and outer with 1480 U-joints, Warn Locking Hubs
Rear locker	Yukon Gear Zip Locker
Front locker	Yukon Gear Zip Locker
Driveshafts (front and rear)	JE Reel 1310
Rear suspension	RockJock 4-inch Johnny Joint suspension system
Front suspension	RockJock 4-inch Johnny Joint suspension system
Rear shock absorbers	Bilstein B8 8100 bypass
Front shock absorbers	Bilstein B8 8100 bypass
Rear control arms	RockJock adjustable Johnny Joint
Front control arms	RockJock adjustable Johnny Joint
Rear track bar	RockJock adjustable Johnny Joint
Front track bar	RockJock adjustable Johnny Joint
Steering tie-rod	Custom with Currie Modular Extreme Duty ends
Steering drag link	Custom with RockJock Modular Extreme Duty ends
Ball joints	F-350/F-450 1 ton
Spindles	Currie Extreme 1-ton unit bearings
Steering knuckles	Currie 1-ton ball joint style
Steering damper	PSC ram assist
Power steering box	PSC
Power steering pump	PSC
Power steering cooler	PSC
Power steering reservoir	PSC
Bracket for steering damper	PSC ram assist bracket

Rear brake rotors	12-inch rotors with zinc-plated caliper bracket
Rear brake calipers	Factory JK rear calipers
Rear brake pads	Stock
Front brake rotors	13-inch vented rotors
Front brake calipers	F-350 Dual-piston calipers
Front brake pads	F-350
Cold air intake	N/A
Catback exhaust	N/A
Battery	Stock
On-board compressor	Yukon Zip Locker Compact
Radiator	Stock
Transmission cooler	Stock
Exterior cooling	N/A
Rear bumper	Rugged Ridge HD
Tire carrier	Rugged Ridge Spartacus HD
Front bumper	Rugged Ridge HD
Winch	NovaWinch Pro 12500
Winch link	Factor 55
Auxiliary fluid storage	Daystar CamCan
Engine/transmission skidplate	Rock Hard 4x4
Gas tank skidplate	Rock Hard 4x4
Transfer case skidplate	Rock Hard 4x4
Fenders	Rugged Ridge steel tube fenders
Rock sliders	Rock Slide Engineering slider steps
On-board air	PowerTank 10 pound with cage mount
Tailgate security storage	Tuffy Tailgate Lockbox
Trunk security storage	Tuffy Deluxe Enclosure
Auxiliary lighting	Ultra Vison
Roll cage	Rock Hard 4x4
Navigation	Magellan TRX 7
Interior storage	Rugged Ridge Molle Storage Bag System
Radio	Midland MXT115 GMRS
FM/Ham radio	Rugged Race Radio Handheld
GMRS antenna	Midland
Jack	Hi-Lift Extreme 48 inch
Ground anchor	PullPal
Extraction boards	MaxTrax
Recovery kit	Factor 55, Hi-Lift, Rugged Ridge
Auxiliary Switches	Rough Country MLC-6 Light Controller

Quinn Thomas's 2020 Gladiator JT Rubicon

Year/Model	2020 Gladiator Rubicon
Engine	3.6L Pentastar V-6
Transmission	8-speed automatic
Transfer case	Rock-Trac NV241 4.0:1
Tires	Nexen Roadian MTX
Wheels	Raceline 17 x 9 Hostage
Rear axle housing	Stock Dana 44
Front axle housing	Stock Dana 44
Rear ring and pinion	Yukon 5.13
Front ring and pinion	Yukon 5.13
Rear axles	Stock
Front axles	Stock
Rear locker	Stock
Front locker	Stock
Rear suspension	RockJock 4 inch
Front suspension	RockJock 4 inch
Rear shock absorbers	Fox 2.5 DSC
Front shock absorbers	Fox 2.5 DSC
Rear control arms	RockJock
Front control arms	RockJock
Rear track bar	RockJock
Front track bar	RockJock
Steering tie-rod	Stock
Steering drag link	Stock
Ball joints	Stock
Steering knuckles	Stock
Steering damper	PSC ram assist
Power steering box	PSC Big Bore
Power steering pump	PSC
Power steering cooler	PSC
Power steering reservoir	PSC
Bracket for steering damper	PSC
Rear brake rotors	Mopar
Rear brake calipers	Mopar
Rear brake pads	Mopar
Front brake rotors	Stock
Front brake calipers	Stock
Front brake pads	Stock
Cold air intake	Stock
Catback exhaust	JBA
Auxiliary switch system	SPOD Bantam x 2
Battery	Stock
On-board compressor	ARB Twin on DV8 Bracket
Radiator	Mopar
Transmission cooler	Mopar
Exterior cooling	—
Rear bumper	Rock Hard 4x4
Tire carrier	—
Front bumper	MetalCloak Frame-Built
Winch	Warn 9.5 TL
Winch link	Safety Thimble 2
Auxiliary fluid storage	—

Engine/transmission skidplate	Artec Full Aluminum
Gas tank skidplate	Artec Full Aluminum
Transfer case skidplate	Artec Full Aluminum
Evap relocation	All
Fenders	Genright Aluminum
Rock sliders	Rock Hard 4x4
Auxiliary lighting	IPF 900
Roll cage	Rock Hard 4x4 Sport Cage
Navigation	Samsung tablet with Backcountry Navigator
Interior storage	Tuffy Security
CB radio	Uniden
FM/Ham radio	Yeasu FT8800
CB Antenna	Firestick 36 inch
FM/Ham antenna	Larson NMO 2/70
Jack	ARB
Recovery kit	ARB Premium with winch line extension, tree saver, kinetic strap, and snatch block

Advance Adapters
advanceadapters.com

AEV—American Expedition Vehicles
aev-conversions.com

Afe Power
afepower.com

All J Products
boulderbars.com

ARB USA
arbusa.com

Artec Industries
artecindustries.com

Baja Designs
bajadesigns.com

Banks Power
Gale Banks Engineering
Bankspower.com

Bestop Inc.
bestop.com

BFG Tires
bfgoodrichtires.com

Big Bear Jeep Experience
bigbearjeepexperience.com

Bilstein of America Thyssenkrupp
bilstein.com

BLM
blm.gov

Borla Exhaust
borla.com

California 4-Wheel-Drive Association
cal4wheel.com

California Off-road Vehicle
Association
corva.org

Currie Enterprises, Inc.
currieenterprises.com

Dana Corp.
dana.com/off-highway

Daystar Products Intl
Daystarweb.com

Dynatrac Products Co., Inc.
dynatrac.com

Eaton
eaton.com/Eaton/ProductsSer-
vices/Vehicle/Differentials/index.
htm

Edlebrock
edelbrock.com

Eibach Springs, Inc.
eibach.com

Enersys (Odyssey Batteries)
enersys.com

Factor 55
Factor55.com

4 Wheel Parts
4wheelparts.com

Fox Racing Shox
ridefox.com

Garvin Industries Inc.
Wilderness Racks
wildernessracks.com

Genright Off-Road
genright.com

Hi-Lift
hi-lift.com/hi-lift-jacks

JE Reel Drive Shaft Specialists
Reeldriveline.com

Jeep 4x4 School
Big Bear Lake, CA 92315
jeep4x4school.com

JKS Manufacturing
jksmfg.com

K&N Filters
knfilters.com

Macs Custom Tie Downs
macscustomtiedowns.com

Magellan GPS
magellangps.com

MaxTrax
us.maxtrax.com.au/

Maxxis Tires
maxxis.com

MCE Fenders
Mcefenders.com

MetalCloak
metalcloak.com

Mickey Thompson Tires &
Wheels
mickeythompsontires.com

Midland Radio Corp
midlandusa.com

NEXEN Tire USA
nexentireusa.com

Nitto Tire U.S.A. Inc.
nittotire.com

Novawinch
novawinch.us/collections/off-road

Off-Road Warehouse
Offroadwarehouse.com

PSC Steering
pscmotorsports.com

Poly Performance/Synergy
polyperformance.com

Power Tank
powertank.com

Pull Pal
pullpal.com

Raceline Wheels
racelinewheels.com

Ram Mounts
rammount.com

RockJock 4x4
rockjock4x4.com

Rock Slide Engineering
rockslideengineering.com

Rockhard 4x4
rockhard4x4.com

RBP Wheels
rollingbigpower.com

Rough Country
roughcountry.com

Rugged Radios
ruggedradios.com

Rugged Ridge
ruggedridge.com

Savvy Off-Road
savvyoffroad.com

Spiderweb Shade
spiderwebshade.com

sPOD
4x4spod.com

Strattec (Bolt Locks)
boltlock.com

Tuffy Security Products
tuffyproducts.com

Ultra Vision Lighting
ultra-vision.com.au

US Forest Service
fs.fed.us

ViAir Corp
viaircorp.com

Warn Industries, Inc.
warn.com

Yukon Gear & Axle
yukongear.com